Dedicated to Val, for patiently enduring my rambling mania.

WEST LANCASHIRE WALKS

Michael Smout

Published by Sigma Leisure – an imprint of
Sigma Press, 1 South Oak Lane, Wilmslow, Cheshire SK9 6AR, England.

British Library Cataloguing in Publication Data
A CIP record for this book is available from the British Library.

ISBN: 1-85058-561-X

Typesetting and Design by: Sigma Press, Wilmslow, Cheshire.

Cover photograph: Tarleton Parish Church, as seen from the footpath on Walk 25.

Maps and photographs: Michael Smout

Printed by: MFP Design and Print

PREFACE

Away from the crowded fells and eroded paths of the Lake District, Snowdonia, Yorkshire Dales and other overpopulated areas, there are still acres where few feet tread. West Lancashire and its boundary areas is one such district. Here there is a great variety of walking available in a comparatively small compass, from the coastal strip of Sefton to the higher ground of Parbold and Dalton. There are numerous footpaths from which to choose. The presence of the Leeds to Liverpool canal, which snakes its way through the area, is a great help in linking walks. This has been aided in recent years by the upgrading of the old Aintree to Southport Cheshire Lines railway by Sustrans and Sefton and Lancashire Councils into a route for walkers, cyclists and horses. Sefton Council has also been responsible for the development of the Sefton Coastal Path.

All the walks in this book are of a circular nature. Footpaths were originally means of getting from one place to another, whether from farm to farm or to the railway station. Hence it is sometimes difficult to get a complete circle of paths. Nonetheless, I have tried to keep road sections to a minimum. The maps have been kept as simple as possible, with stiles marked as S, gates as G and footbridges as FB. The written descriptions try to give as much detail as will be helpful. As time goes by, footpath signs are erected or sometimes illegally removed, hedges are rooted up and fences erected, houses built or demolished. So the more route marks that are available, the better. The numbers on the map refer to the parallel point in the description.

The Grid references enable a point to be found from the Ordnance Survey map. The first three numbers given refer to the numbers along the top and bottom of the map. The second three refer to the numbers along each side of the map. The times given for the duration of the walks are very approximate. Time taken will vary depending upon the number of walkers, the weather and other factors. It is always advisable to have the relevant Pathfinder Ordnance Survey map with you as a back-up. But even with this, it is possible that some paths have been diverted since publication. If this is so, the diversion of the path will normally be clearly shown on the ground. For up to date information, it is possible to consult the Definitive Map at the appropriate Council Offices. With regard to transport, train times and bus times and routes are subject to such constant change, that any information given would soon be out of date. Up to date information on buses is usually available at bus stations, local libraries and council offices. Merseytravel covers a big section of the area. Information can be obtained from Merseytravel on 0151-236 7676.

Landowners have responsibilities to maintain footpaths. Walkers, on the other hand, need to ensure that they stay on the paths, shut gates behind them and, in general, act sensibly.

The Ramblers' Association has over 100,000 members. Its local groups organise local walks and try to ensure that the laws regarding footpaths are implemented. We consider the footpaths as an important part of our national heritage. I have tried to ensure that the footpaths used in this book are free of obstruction and properly maintained and will continue to monitor them. If, by chance, in the course of one of the walks, you happen to encounter a problem, then the most effective action is to write to or ring up the Rights of Way Officer of the appropriate local council. If you would like more information about the Ramblers' Association, contact Mr. Geoff Wright, Secretary of the West Lancs R.A. on 01772-812034. The West Lancs Footpaths Group can be contacted through its Secretary, Mrs Margaret Smith on 01695-422682.

My thanks are due to Margaret Sadler for transferring my typescript onto disk so speedily and carefully.

It is my hope that the walks outlined in this book will bring much pleasure and enjoyment to those who undertake them.

Michael Smout

Contents

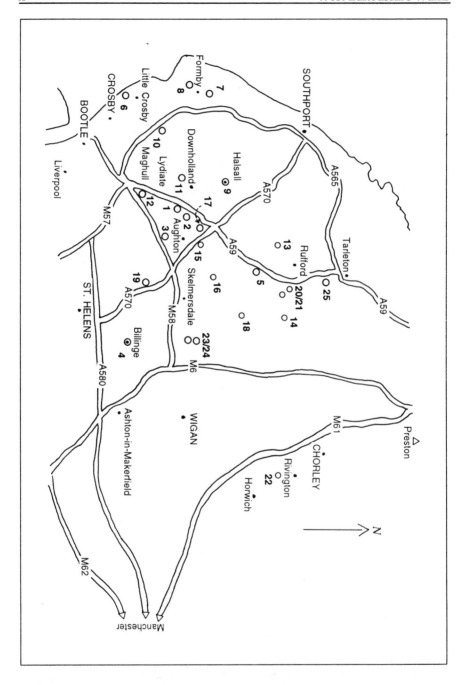

Walk 1

Aughton (1)

St Michael's Church, Aughton Old Hall and Walsh Hall are historic buildings included in this walk. It is an easy stroll through the rich agricultural land of Aughton and Downholland.

Route: St Michael's, Aughton — Walsh Hall — Rimmer's Bridge — St Michael's, Aughton.

Start: The car park at St Michael's Church, Aughton. Grid reference: 392 054.

Distance: 5 or 3½ miles.

Duration: 3½ or 2½ hours.

Map: SD20/30

By train: Town Green Station, on the Liverpool-Ormskirk Merseyrail line, is half a mile away. The start of the walk is reached via Bold Lane and Church Lane.

By car: Aughton is on the A59 between Maghull and Ormskirk. St Michael's church is reached by turning off the A59 along St Michael's Road.

Refreshments: The Stanley Arms, opposite the church, and the Scarisbrick Arms by the canal bridge at Downholland.

---

1. *The walk starts from the car park.* Opposite the car-park is the church. The oldest part of the building is the south aisle, which dates from the fourteenth century. The lower parts of the walls contain stone from the Norman Church, the old doorway of which can be seen behind the buttress by the present porch. The eighteenth century sundial in the church-yard has an inscription 'Remember only the sunny hours'. Walk back up St Michael's Road towards the A59, passing the Stanley Arms and Aughton Old Hall on the left. The Stanley Arms dates from the late eighteenth century and originally served as a stopping place for the Liverpool to Preston stage coach. Aughton Old Hall was one of the original manor houses. In front of the house are the remains of a fifteenth century pele-tower.

St Michael's Church

Just after a bungalow on the left and opposite Aughton Springs, turn left by the signpost into the yard of Old Hall Farm. Continue ahead, with the house on your right, through a gate into a field. Turn immediately left through another gate.

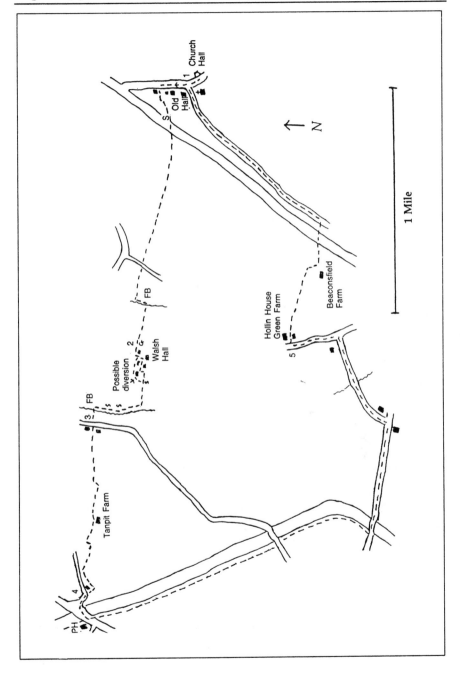

Bear to the right across the field to the stile by the gate onto the dual carriageway. The path you are following probably goes back to Saxon times, when it was part of the route from Town Green through Halsall and the marshes to the sea.

Having crossed the busy road, the wide track goes through the middle of a very large field. It then becomes a narrow ridgeway path towards a small clump of trees in the distance. Across the narrow metal road, keep to the ditch on your right. Turn left at the corner of the field to reach the footbridge over the stream. Over the stile, keep the hedge on your right as you make towards Walsh Hall in the distance.

2. *Through the gate, pass the barn on the left.* Turn left and the Hall is immediately ahead. A small detour is to turn left for a hundred metres or so. To the right you will see the remains of the moat and a small part of the ancient hall which was demolished in 1891. Return back to the original point with the present hall facing you.

Go into the yard, with the house on your left. Turn right through the farm out-buildings, then left between the stables. Turn right along the track *(note that a diversion is planned around the front of the farm buildings)* which brings you to a fence and a stile in a few metres. Go straight across the middle of the field towards a bridge over a stream. Do not go over it, but proceed to the right. Keeping the stream on the left, go over two stiles and soon reach a footbridge. Cross this and go straight ahead, with the fence on the right. This brings you to Green Lane.

3. *To shorten the walk,* go left along the road until you eventually reach Rimmer's Bridge across the canal. At this point the longer walk route is picked up again.

For the longer walk, cross Green Lane and follow the footpath sign ahead between the houses. This is a good grass track and carries on until it passes Tanpit Farm on the left. It now becomes a well-used farm track. As it swings sharply to the right, the right of way is to the right-hand side of the cottage on your left. Turn right into the field and keep the hedge on the right. At the corner of the field do not go straight ahead onto the road, because it is not a right of way. This goes left along the edge of the field, with the hedge to the right. Turn right on reaching the small council depot. Reach the road through the small gate by the cottage.

4. *Follow the road to the left* and then left again over the canal bridge. Descend the steps onto the tow path. Here is a seat to take a rest. There is also a pub at the bridge for refreshments.

   From here is a walk down the tow path. Pass Rimmer's Bridge, which is of the swing variety. Eventually reach a road bridge. Walk to the left down Pygons Hill Lane and turn left into Suddell Lane. Over Suddell brook bridge, turn left at the T-Junction.

5. *The road reaches Hollin House Green Farm.* Turn right between the farm buildings and then straight across the large field, aiming for a corner of the hedge in the far distance. On reaching this, you are on a track, which leads towards Beaconsfield Farm.

   Do not turn left along the farm road towards the A59. The right of way is along the edge of the field, which a hedge divides from the farm road. Cross the A59 and turn left along the minor road back to St Michael's Church.

Walk 2

Aughton (2)

Passing by ancient Moor Hall and Quakers Burial Ground, this walk is a circuit through farm land to the east of Aughton.

Route: Village Hall – Gerard Hall – Quakers' Graveyard – Village Hall.

Start: The Village Hall car park, Aughton. Grid reference: 401 056.

Distance: 4½ miles.

Duration: 2 hours.

Map: SD40/50 plus a minute part of 20/30

By train: Town Green Station is on the Liverpool to Ormskirk Merseyrail Line.

By car: From the A59, turn right at the roundabout (map reference: 394 062), signposted Town Green Station. After half a mile, the Village Hall is on the right at the T-Junction.

Refreshments: The Cockbeck pub (formerly the Railway Inn) near the station bridge.

1. From the car-park, turn right along the road and, almost immediately, left at the T-Junction. Go over the railway bridge and turn right down Middlewood Road. Continue to the end of the road, with Belvedere Park housing estate on the right. Carry on ahead onto the footpath. Follow it, ignoring tracks to the left, as it bends to the right and eventually to the left to meet the road.

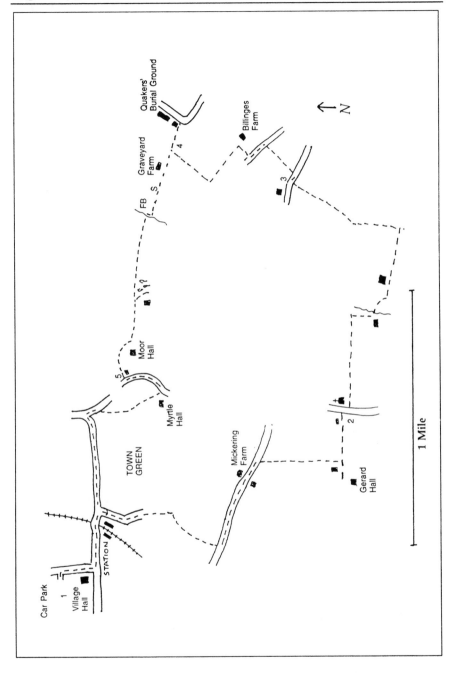

Walk left down the road. After the houses, the road has some sharp bends. Beyond Mickering Farm, pass the first signpost to the right. The second sign to the right is placed on the opposite side of the road. It is near to a small nature area managed by the Lancashire Nature Conservancy Trust. Turn right through the fields, following the telegraph poles, to reach Gerard Hall farm. Just after the first barn, turn left along the farm access road. Looking back, it is possible to see the old farm house.

2. *The access road reaches a junction* with the main road, almost opposite St Mary's Roman Catholic Church. Until it was built in 1823, the Catholics of the area worshipped at Moor Hall, passed later in the walk. Turn right in front of the church. Then turn left, immediately after the church, at the signpost. The path goes along the left edge of the field and then that of a second one. The fields, plus more of the walk, were being turned into a golf course, but progress seems to have come to a halt.

At the end of the second field, go right, along the edge of the stream. At the access drive to the house, turn left and down the track which led through the former farm buildings. This was, until recent times, Mossock Hall Farm. Before demolition Mossock Hall, nearby, was famous for its ghosts, especially the mysterious lady in the green dress. This track continues until a hedge is reached. As the track goes to the right, turn left along the edge of the field. In a short while, this crosses into another field. The path, which the farmer keeps well-marked, goes across the field to the road.

3. *Turn right along the road.* After a short distance, turn left at the signpost across another well-maintained path. This soon reaches another lane. Turn left and soon right up the track to Billinges Farm. Do not go into the yard, but turn left along a track just before it. At the end of the field, turn right, keeping

the hedge to the right. At the end of this field, carry on along a narrow path to the right of the fence.

4. *At the end of the path, as it reaches the lane,* make a short detour to the right and then round the corner to the left on the road. Here is the Quakers Burial Ground on Graveyard Lane. This was purchased by the much persecuted group of Christians in 1655. Over 200 are buried here. There are no stones or name markings to locate particular graves. This was a deliberate policy of the Quakers. Also to be seen is an old mounting stone. The lead coffins meant that no trees or bushes have grown over the actual grave area.

Quaker burial ground

Go back on to the lane to the right, to the signpost at which you emerged onto the lane. Go straight ahead, passing a farm on the right. Go over a stile and continue forward to reach a stream. Turn right and then soon left over the footbridge. Walk on, with the hedge on the right. This is a long stretch that passes a stile in the hedge. At the end of the field, the track continues, with a plantation on the left. With a house in front, it then bears right and left onto a lane.

Turn right along the lane. On the left are the grounds of Moor Hall. The Hall was built by Peter Stanley in the sixteenth century. It remained in the hands of the Stanley family until 1840. Over the doorway were written the words, 'Pray ye for the good estate of Peter Stanley Esq. and Cecily his wife, with their children, who caused this work to be made in the year of our Lord 1566'. Here, in earlier days of persecution, Catholic families met in secret to celebrate the Mass. A priest would arrive at midnight and the service would be said in an upper room. The Hall is privately owned.

5. *At the end of the lane, turn left along the road.* Just before Myrtle Hall, go right at the signpost down the track. After a while, it runs to the left of houses and then, as it bears to the right, becomes a concrete path. At the end of the path, turn left along the road and soon left again along Town Green Lane. This will bring you back over the railway bridge to turn right to the Village Hall.

Walk 3

Bickerstaffe

*A walk through the flat agricultural land of Bickerstaffe,
never far from the busy M58. It overlaps walk No.2 by about
a quarter of a mile.*

Route: Royal Oak – Little Wood – Graveyard Lane – Royal Oak.

Start: Pumping Station, Royal Oak. Grid reference: 419 034.

Distance: 5½ or 4 miles.

Duration: 3 or 2 hours.

Map: SD40/50.

By train: None

By car: Turn right off the A506 at Royal Oak. Grid reference: 417 037.
Just past the pumping station, there is room to park on the road to the
left.

Refreshments: None.

1. *From the pumping station,* follow the road over the motorway
   bridge. Turn first left down the road between the houses. As
   it swings sharply to the right, the waymarker on the post on
   the right-hand side, directs you along the right-hand side of
   the grounds of the house. Continue with the hedge to the left
   and follow the bank of the stream along the field, until
   reaching the bend of a metal road.

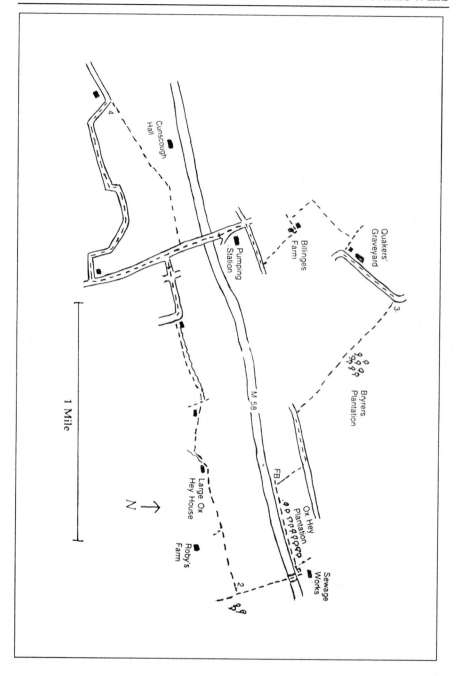

Pumping Station at Royal Oak

Go ahead along the road, passing a house to the right. At the bridge, there is a gate with a notice 'Private Road' on it. A footpath sign points to the left. Walk along the near bank of the stream. Passing to the rear of the farm at Large Ox Hey House, pick up the cart track that comes from the farm. This continues in the same direction that you are already walking. Pass a track coming from the left and also one that goes to the right to Roby's Farm. All the while the track is parallel to the motorway.

Follow the track into the next field. After a while the stream bends to the right and the way ahead is through the middle of fields, with the occasional length of hedge on the right. Bickerstaffe parish church can be seen in the distance. At the corner of Small Wood, the main track goes at right angles.

2. *Turn left along the narrow well-used path to the left of the* *hedge.* Cross the footbridge over the motorway. Descending from it, the sewage plant is immediately in front of you. After a few metres the main path goes right over a footbridge. Instead, carry on ahead to the right of the hedge and wire fence very close to the motorway. This is Ox Hey Plantation. After walking the length of the woodland, there is a short section of gorseland, with a wooden fence on the left.

At the stream, turn right across the footbridge into the field. Walk along the right-hand side of the field towards the house on the other side of the road. Emerge on the road by the footpath sign. Turn left along the pavement. Look, after a few hundred metres, for a sign on the right-hand side of the road. Walk through the field on the right-hand side of the hedge towards Bryer's Plantation. The path goes along the front of the woodland and continues to the right of the hedge in the next field.

3. *The path arrives at Graveyard Lane.* Turn left along the road. Just past the Quakers' Graveyard, turn right at the houses. Further information about the graveyard is given in Walk no. 2. The lane has private road notices, but it is a public right of way for walkers. Turn left at the signpost, walking to the left of the fence. In the next field, walk to the right of the hedge. Turn left along the track to Billinge's Farm. Turn left through the farmyard. Coming into the field at the back of the farm, turn right along the back of the farm buildings. Then follow the line of the light coloured poles. The path reaches the road to the left of the house.

At the road, go to the right, passing the few houses of Royal Oak. Finally, turn left into Simonswood Lane and back to the start.

To lengthen the walk, continue on over the motorway bridge again. On the other side, look for a sign on the right. Descend the steps and then walk ahead through the field on the right of the hedge. At the end of the field, cross the ditch. Go straight on through a short stretch of gorse into a field. Walk to the left of the wide gorse hedge, soon picking up a track. After passing a copse of small trees on the left, the track veers gradually to the left.

The track continues for about half a mile. Cunscough Hall can be seen over to the right.

4. *At Hesketh Farm, turn left along the narrow metal road.* After a while, it turns sharp left. Follow this road, through hedges and fields, until, after passing a derelict house on the right at a sharp left-hand bend, it meets a T-Junction, with a house on the left corner. Turn left and follow the road back across the motorway bridge to the starting point. On this last stretch there is no pavement, until a few hundred metres before the bridge, so care needs to be taken.

Walk 4

Billinge

Billinge Beacon is a well known landmark included in this walk round the Billinge area. The part of the walk up to the Beacon is a long steady pull.

Route: St Aidan's Church — Blackley Hurst Hall — Carr Mill — Billinge Beacon — St Aidan's Church.

Start: St Aidan's Parish Church, Billinge. Grid reference: 533 007.

Distance: 4½ miles.

Duration: 2 hours.

Maps SJ49/59 and SD40/50.

By train: None

By car: Come from Liverpool direction along the A580 East Lancs Road. After passing under the M6, turn left to Billinge at the roundabout. Grid reference: 509 973.

Refreshments: Eagle and Child and the Stork, Billinge and Masons Arms, Chadwick Green.

---

1. *From the church, walk along Newton Road.* After the houses end on the right, continue and turn right at the footpath sign, with a small factory on the opposite side of the road. This is a wide track that leads towards Blackley Hurst Hall, amongst the trees in the distance. On reaching the much renovated hall, follow the track as it veers to the right. Most of the tracks in this area are old ones which were used to reach the now defunct colliery.

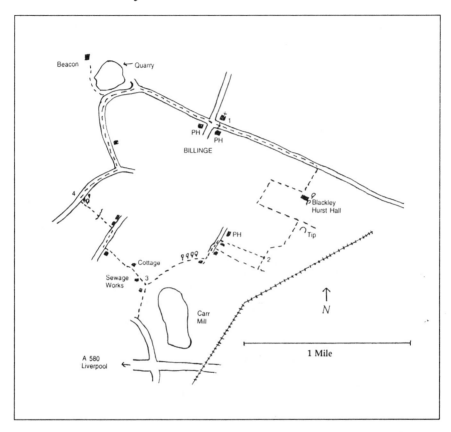

With houses across the field ahead of you, do not take the narrow path that leads towards them, but follow the main track around to the left. This reaches a T-Junction. Turn left down the lane towards the pit mound. This is all that is now left of the old Blackley Hurst Colliery. Before turning right in front of the mound, notice that the path that goes straight ahead is made of well-fashioned stone. Follow the path to the right as it gradually descends, with the St Helens gas holder a prominent feature in the landscape ahead. The way is through open fields, with a few trees on the right. Eventually the track veers right and then left. It then runs alongside wooden fencing.

2. *On coming to a gate,* which leads to a path between fencing to the right, there is a choice of ways. If a visit to the Masons Arms is required, turn right through the gap by the gate and walk between the fences. As the fences end, look to a tree ahead. A notice tells you that the path is between the tree and the fence to the right. Continue along the back of a building on the left to arrive at the road. Turn left along the road until reaching the Masons Arms on the left. From here, continue along the road, until arriving at a footpath sign on the left, by a house. You have now rejoined the other route.

If a visit to the Masons Arms is not needed, do not turn right by the gate, but carry on ahead down the narrower track. This reaches a T-Junction. Turn right and follow the path through the field, until it arrives at the road along a narrow length between two houses. At the road, where the alternative route rejoins, turn left and very soon there is a double sign pointing straight on and to the right. Go to the right, with the house on the left. The wide path goes through trees and emerges into open country, as it becomes a harder surface.

3. *At the junction of paths, it is possible to go ahead to Carr Mill Dam,* which is a popular local leisure spot. Otherwise, turn right. The lane goes through a slight dip buy the sewage works and passes Otters Swift cottage to the right. After passing other houses on the right, go through a farm to the main road.

Cross the road and turn right. After about a hundred metres, a rather old sign stands back from the road, by the first house in the row. Turn left, along the edge of gardens and, later, a hedge. The path dips over a stream to join a much wider one coming in from the left. Keep straight ahead. As the hedge on the right ends, the track is going across an open field. The wide track swings to the left, but go ahead on a narrower path towards the copse and pond. By the trees, the path arrives at a road.

Otter's Swift cottage

4. *Turn right and walk along the pavement.* Do not turn left at the road with the seat on the corner. Continue round the sharp bend. The next road on the left is a road which carries lorries to the quarry on the hill. Notices make it clear that the road is not for cars and general traffic. Go up the road and follow it as it veers left at the houses and footpath sign. This is a long steady climb, but compensated for by the surrounding panoramic views.

As the road bends to the right, turn left before the sub-station. Follow the path up the hill, with the quarry fence to the right. From the summit take time to admire the views. Come back down the same path. At the road, turn left and follow round the left-handed bend. You are now confronted by the main entrance to the quarry. At first sight, it looks as if there is no way of escape. But, by going to the right-hand side of the road, a wide track downhill will be seen. After a few metres it is fenced across, but room for the footpath is left to the right of the fencing.

The path follows along the edge of the fence straight into Beacon Lane. Follow the lane all the way down until the parish church is reached.

Walk 5

Burscough

This is an easy flat walk, including canal, footpaths and two short sections of road.

Route: Lord Street – Top Locks – Crabtree Farm – Lord Street.

Start: Lord Street car park Burscough. Grid reference: 444 122.

Distance: 4½ miles.

Duration: 2 hours.

Map: SD41/51.

By train: Burscough Bridge station is on the Southport – Manchester line.

By car: Coming from the Liverpool direction on the A59, turn first right after the canal bridge, then right again into the car park.

Refreshments: Red Lion.

---

1. *Proceed back to the A59.* After crossing the road, make towards the canal bridge and onto the tow-path. As the houses come to an end on the left and Ainscough's mill is passed to the right, go under the railway bridge. The mill was built by Hugh Ainscough in 1858 to complement an earlier one erected in Parbold. American wheat was loaded directly onto the barges in Liverpool docks and brought up the canal. The unloading bays in front of the mill are still clearly seen.

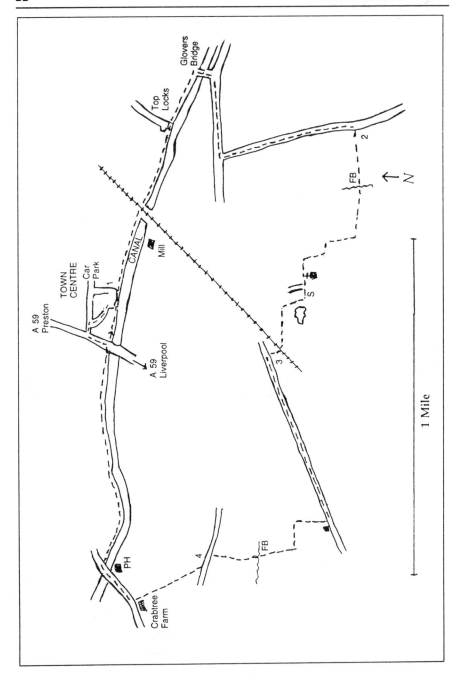

Continue along until Top Locks is reached. This is a beautiful little spot. Here was created the first canal junction in Lancashire. It was opened in 1781 between the Rufford branch and the main canal. It has two locks, a dry dock, toll house and canal workers' cottages.

From Top Locks continue along the tow path, until Glovers Bridge is reached. Cross the bridge, and then the road onto the pavement on the opposite side. This is Briars Lane. Walk to the right and, after a while, take the first road on the left into Flax Lane.

2. *After a quarter of a mile*, turn right at a signpost onto a footpath, just before the lane gets to the Ellerbrook. Follow the path, which stays on the higher side of the ground, although it is obvious that people also walk illegally on the lower side. Cross a footbridge and continue along the edge of the field. Before reaching a wood, the path turns to the right to follow a twisting wide farm track until it reaches the Catholic church. The church and presbytery were built between 1815 and 1819, alongside the old Burscough Hall. Follow the path, with the church to the left and the school to the right. Go ahead through an old stone stile, between an avenue of trees, shortly reaching a more modern stile. Follow the path to the left and then round to the right. It drops down some wooden steps to the Platta Lane lake.

Follow the path along the right edge of the lake and then straight ahead, with the gardens of houses on the right. The path then goes left through an avenue of trees to join a well-used path coming in from the left. Go right and, in a few metres, cross the railway bridge leading to the A59.

3. *Cross the road, turning left along the A59.* Just before reaching the Red Lion, turn right at a footpath sign before the Derby works. The path goes between the buildings and then along the side of a hedge. Turn left along a wider track, with a tall

hedge to the right. The main track goes ahead, but turn right along the next hedge on a narrow path, keeping the hedge on the left. At the junction of paths at the end of the field, keep straight ahead on a wider track, crossing a footbridge and eventually reaching Higgins Lane.

4. *Across the road, turn left and, after a few metres,* take the track to the right, which arrives on Crabtree Lane, to the right of Crabtree Farm. Here turn right along the road to the swing bridge. Over the bridge, turn right along the tow-path and back to the A59 at the next canal bridge.

Renovated quay at Burscough Bridge

Walk 6

Crosby

Although close to the built up area of Crosby, the walk is
mainly rural. It includes the villages of Little Crosby and
Hightown and a section of the Sefton Coastal Path.

Route: Hall Road Station – Blundellsands – Little Crosby – Hightown – Coastal Path – Hall Road Station.

Start: Hall Road Station, Blundellsands. Grid reference: 305 006

Distance: 6 miles.

Duration: 3 hours.

Map: SD20/30.

By train: Hall Road station is on the Merseyrail Liverpool – Southport line. It is possible also to pick the walk up at Hightown station, the next one towards Southport.

By car: There is parking on the road to the station. This is reached by taking the first main turn to the right (St Michael's Road), from the B5193, three-quarters of a mile south of Little Crosby. Then, at the roundabout, turn right into Manor Road and, at a 90 degree left turn, into Hall Road East.

Refreshments: In the centre of Hightown and at the car-park by the Coastguard Station.

---

1. *From the station, go back along Hall Road East,* admiring the

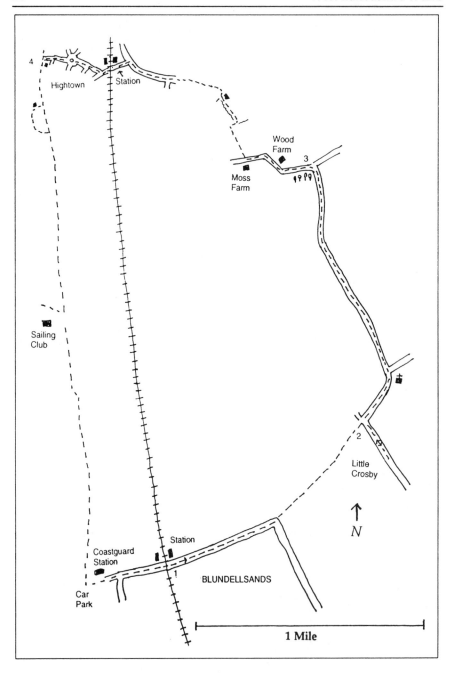

4

Hightown

Station

Wood
Farm

3

Moss
Farm

Sailing
Club

2

Little
Crosby

↑
N

Station

Coastguard
Station

BLUNDELLSANDS

1

Car
Park

1 Mile

prosperous houses of Blundellsands. Where the road turns right into Manor Road, go straight ahead along Dibb Lane, following the bridle-path sign to Little Crosby. The path is wide and, after a hedge to the right, continues, with a ditch on either side, towards the village ahead.

2. *Reaching the road*, after passing an open grass space on the right, it is worth a small detour along the road to the right into Little Crosby village. A little way along the road, on the right, is the ancient cross. Almost opposite is a crucifix, erected in memory of Francis Nicholas Blundell, the squire, 1880 – 1936. The local landowners, the Blundell family, lived for centuries at Crosby Hall, which is now in private hands.

A little further on, the left, are some whitewashed cottages. A plaque on one of them tells us that this is a conservation area of the cottages and farm buildings of the Blundell of Crosby

Estate cottages, Little Crosby

estate. Opposite to these, the date 1669 can be seen above the door of one of the cottages.

Retrace your steps to point 2. Now go along the road straight ahead towards Little Crosby Roman Catholic Church of St Mary. This is a traditionally strong area of northern Catholicism. Many of its adherents were persecuted for their faith in centuries past. Turn left along Moss Lane. This is a busy stretch of road, so keep well into the grass verge on the right. On reaching Flea Moss Wood on the left, the road swings to the right. Immediately after the wood, turn left by the Farm Shop sign, along Gorsey Lane.

3. *Follow the narrow road as it veers to the right by Wood Farm.* After a turn to the left, it reaches Moss Farm. With the farm buildings on the left, turn right, by the footpath sign, along the farm track across the fields. Soon there is a ditch to the right. The track goes to the right. As it swings back again to the left, the right of way is no longer along the track, but parallel to it on the other side of the ditch. The path passes between the grounds of a house to the right and a line of trees to the left, to arrive at a lane.

Turn right and follow the lane as it swings to the left. Pass a sports field on the left and then a cricket ground on the right. At the end of the lane, go straight ahead along the road, passing Elmcroft Lane on the left. Turn left into Alt Road and arrive, in a few hundred metres, at Hightown station. Cross the railway line by means of the bridge. Turn right into Lower Alt Road by the sign indicating the direction of the Coastal Footpath. On the right is a small shop selling refreshments.

Go straight ahead to the roundabout. Cross directly ahead and continue into the second half of Lower Alt Road. After passing Riverside to the left and the 'No entry' for cars signs, turn left beyond the Alt Centre.

4. *Then, almost immediately,* take the path on the right that leads alongside the River Alt. This is part of the Sefton Coastal path. Soon the river bends away to the right and the path continues towards the dunes.

It is worth making a small diversion from the main path towards a small brick building on the right. Follow a path to the left of this onto the beach and, after a few hundred metres, follow the path through the gully to the left of the large outlet pipe, back onto the main path. There is a maze of pathways in the area, but fortunately Sefton Council have indicated the way with white topped markers. There is always one in sight, so the path is easy to follow. At one point, it emerges by the Blundellsands Sailing Club. Just to the right is a short path to the beach, marked 'Submerged Forest'. This is worth the detour to see the remains of the ancient forest of centuries ago, eventually claimed by the sea.

Cross directly across the Sailing Club car park to the continuation of the path. At this point, there is an estate of houses over to the left. Continue to follow the marker posts. The last one is at a point where the path bears left. Look, to the left, towards a marker post with a white top. This bears a yellow arrow pointing to the right. Follow this to another similar post, which points the way along a wide track. With the sea to the right, follow this track, passing a new sewage disposal plant on the left and eventually reaching the Coastguard Station. By this is a large car park, with extensive views across the Mersey estuary towards the Wirral and Wales. If the tide is right, it is possible to see ships either coming into or leaving the port of Liverpool. There is usually a refreshment point here. Toilet facilities are also available.

The Coastguard Station replaced the old site in Formby. Walk from the car park, passing the Coastguard Station. At the road, go ahead down Hall Road West to arrive back at the railway station.

Walk 7

Formby (1)

*The walk includes an ancient path and part of the Sefton
Coastal Path. It is mostly flat and mainly through dunes and
woodland.*

Route: Freshfield Station — Fisherman's Path — Cornerstone Walk —
Squirrel Walk — Freshfield Station.

Start: Freshfield Station. Grid reference: 292 083.

Distance: 3 miles.

Duration: 1½ hours.

Map: SD20/30

By train: Freshfield station is on the Merseyrail Liverpool — Southport
Northern line.

By car: Freshfield Station is in Victoria Road. There is usually room to
park a car in the first part of Montagu Road, next to the station car park.

Refreshments: Available at the shop by the station. During summer
months, there is an ice-cream van at Squirrel Walk.

---

1. *From the station, walk along Montagu Road,* which is adjacent
to the station car park. As the car park ends on the left, there
is a choice of following the bridle-path on the left, or continuing straight along the metal road. If the latter, soon ignore the
right turn and continue ahead at the 'no entry' sign. The two
ways come together at a bridleway sign pointing ahead. After

Fisherman's Close on the right, there is a second sign. The third sign points to a path to the right. Continue ahead here.

Continue to follow the track, with the railway fence on the left, and after the last house, trees and then short wooden stakes on the right. On reaching the gate to the railway crossing, proceed with caution. Trains pass about eight times an hour, so it is a dangerous place. The Samaritans poster indicates that this had been a place of disaster on a number of occasions.

2. *The notice on the other side of the crossing* indicates that you are going on to the Fisherman's Path. This had been in use for hundreds of years from times when fishing was an important

Beach marker

local industry. At the start, the path goes through part of Formby Golf Course, so take no notice of the cross paths, which are used by golfers. After a while, arrive at a notice board, where the woodland commences. There is a path to the right, but continue ahead through mainly fir trees. Then begin a long gradual descent towards the shore through trees and shrubs. After passing a small log amphitheatre on the left, the track becomes sandy and, soon after, narrows, with wooden railings to the right.

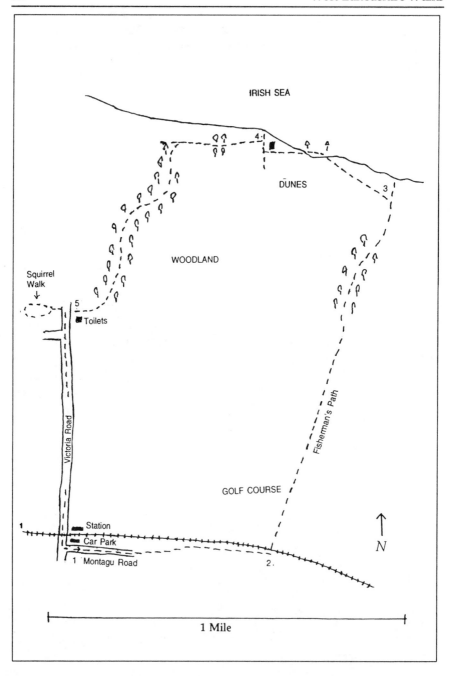

IRISH SEA

DUNES

WOODLAND

Squirrel
Walk

5

Toilets

Victoria Road

Fisherman's Path

GOLF COURSE

N

Station

Car Park

1 Montagu Road

2.

1 Mile

3. *At a wooden litter box,* bear left rather than go straight on towards the shore. On the right is a faded Sefton Coastal Path sign. From here the track surface alternates between hard and sandy. To the right are views of the dunes and occasional glimpses of the sea. As on all of the walk, white topped stakes help to define the way. When the path eventually reaches the beach, there is a notice board on the left and an orange beacon marker on the beach. Go onto the beach and walk left along it to the next marker. On good days, there are views across the water to Blackpool Tower in the distance.

By the marker, turn left up the short steep incline from the beach and right, back onto the Coastal Path. The other paths going inland towards the woods are to be ignored. Passing along the way a wire fence on the right, the path meets a wide one used by cars, at a T-Junction. Turn right onto this and immediately having passed a derelict building on the right and a path on the left, turn left along the track marked Cornerstone Way.

4. *The track passes through a copse of small trees.* Again there are tracks off to the left and right along the way. Soon this main track bears to the left, as another one goes straight ahead. Again the white topped markers are useful. From here the track continues in snake like fashion, but since it has a hard surface, it is easy to follow.

5. *The path emerges near the Victoria Road entrance to the National Trust site.* Here, will be found an information board and toilets. Across the other side of the wide road will be found Squirrel Walk. This is a red squirrel reserve, but it is not always possible to guarantee the appearance of the squirrels, particularly on very hot days.

Walk back down Victoria Road. This full of imposing and largely unaltered houses from the era of the 1930s. Finally, arrive back at Freshfield Station.

Walk 8

Formby (2)

Asparagus fields are not all that common. We come across them on this walk through the dunes close to southern Formby.

Route: St Luke's Church – Formby Point – Wicks Wood – St Luke's Church.

Start: St Luke's Church, Formby. Grid reference: 282 067.

Distance: 4 miles.

Duration: 2½ hours.

Map: SD20/30.

By train: None

By car: Continue three-quarters of a mile west from Formby Station. The road turns sharply left into Church Road. St Luke's Church is on the right.

Refreshments: None.

---

1. *From St Luke's Church, turn right into Lifeboat Road.* The church dates from the middle of the nineteenth century. At that time, it was isolated in the sandhills. The graves of the Formby family are in the graveyard, as are the old market cross and stocks of Formby village.

   For the first part of Lifeboat Road, it is possible to walk on a path on the edge of the woodland. Back on the road, pass the caravan park on the left. A car park, with admission charge, is on the right. Continue along the road until it turns to sand and begins to rise sharply. Before this turn left through some posts and go on towards more posts ahead. Through these, follow the path with the white topped markers. This area is the Ravenmeols Local Nature Reserve. At the third marker is a junction of paths. Here, turn right and again follow the white markers as the path starts to go uphill towards the dunes. As it passes through the dunes, it is sunken for a short length, until it arrives on the beach by a beacon.

The dunes at Formby

2. Turn right to walk along the beach. At the next beacon, notice the ruins of the old lifeboat station, not improved by the vandals. This was the first lifeboat station in the country. Proceed along the beach and, at the fourth beacon, turn right up the board-walk. Continue along the path. At the junction, take the path going to the left. This eventually goes along the right-hand side of a wood.

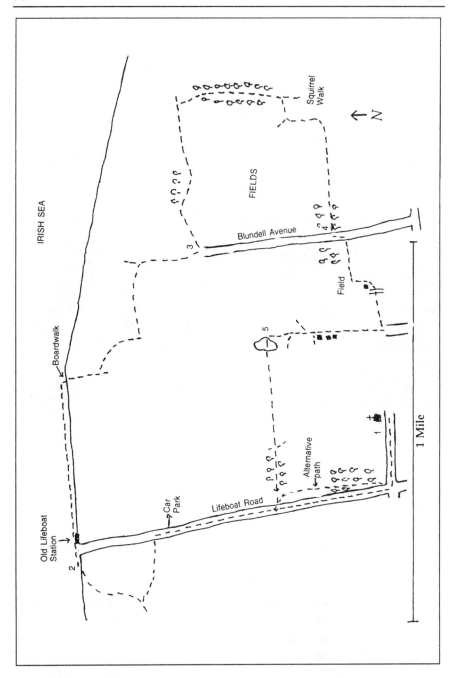

Before the end of the wood, look for a Formby Point notice, with a small coastal footpath sign on the post. Here, turn left through the wood. The path comes into the open and then through more wood. Soon after coming out of the second wood, there is a signpost, indicating the Blundell path. Turn right, away from the coast. The path has, at first, a surface of wood shavings. Ignore the path to the right and left and continue until coming to a lone lamp-post at the end of a metal road.

3. *Turn left along the track.* On the right are fields used for growing asparagus. At a sign for Nicotine Wood, bear to the right. The path keeps to the edge of the fields, until it crosses more open heathland. It keeps moving to the right, until reaching the 'Woodland Path' signpost. Turn right and follow the path into the wood. The path winds through the trees. Do not take any other paths to the left.

On reaching a path to the right, there is a sign, the reverse of which says 'Woodland Path'. Go along this path and then first right. Follows this down the boards and then turn left. At the top of this path, you are in Squirrel Walk. Turn right and follow the path through the woodland. Then, with an open field to the right, it passes through two sets of low stakes, with another path coming from the left.

Keep straight on, with a notice on the fencing to the left announcing 'Private Lane', to arrive at Blundell Avenue.

4. *Turn left and, immediately after the woods end on the right,* turn right down a wooden step. The path runs through open heathland, with the woods to the right. Do not take the track to the right into the woods, but go ahead. The path then runs alongside more asparagus fields, until it bears left towards a house.

By the house, the path runs diagonally across towards a tall hedge by a lane. Cross the lane and take the path that runs parallel to the wood until it bears a little to the right. It then meets Wicks Lane at the corner of the wood. Turn right along the sandy lane, shaded by trees. Do not turn right down the track by the wooden pillar. Keep straight on with, first, a school playing field to the left and secondly, a long line of wooden palings at the end of gardens.

As the palings end, do not follow the main track to the right, but go straight on uphill. This path then runs between railings. After a few metres, go right down the flight of wooden steps. On the left is a picnic area with tables. Then comes Dune Lake.

5. *Turn left on the path across the centre of the lake.* Keep on this path as it goes ahead towards low trees in the distance. Do not take paths to the left or right.

When the path arrives at the trees, do not take the track going up the steps to the left, but continue into the wood. From the wood the path emerges onto Lifeboat Road. Turn left and then left again to reach St Luke's Church.

Walk 9

Halsall

An ancient church, an old railway station and the earliest part of the Leeds-Liverpool canal are included in this level walk.

Route: St Cuthbert's Church – Barton Station – Canal – St Cuthbert's Church.

Start: Halsall Church on A567 Liverpool – Southport road. Grid reference: 370 103

Distance: 5 or 4 miles.

Duration: 2½ or 2 hours.

Map: SD20/30 and 21/31

By train: None

By car: Parking available outside Halsall Church.

Refreshments: Saracens Head opposite the church, Kings Arms and Ship Inn at Haskayne.

1. *The walk starts from the ancient parish church of Halsall.* The chancel dates from 1370. Inside look for the figure of the wrestlers on the misericords in the choir stalls. By the tower is the old grammar school dating from 1593. Amongst the variety of gargoyles on the outside of the church is a man seated in a boat. This seems to indicate, that, in centuries past, the sea came in as far as Halsall.

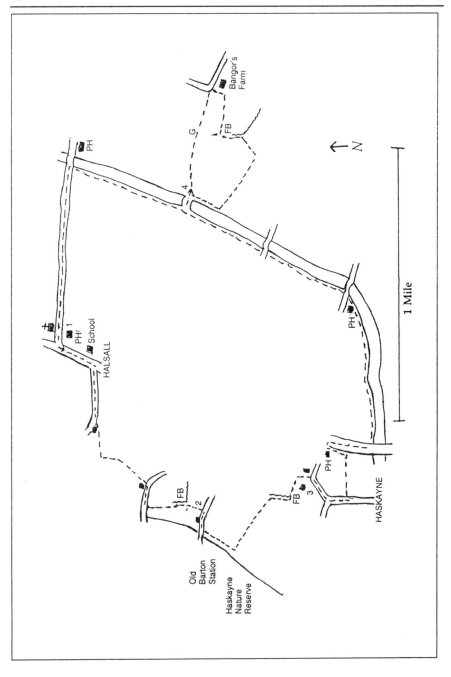

From the church, walk back along the road left towards Liverpool. Just beyond the school, turn right into Carr Moss Lane. As the houses on the left come to a stop and just before a bungalow, the road bends to the right. Turn left at the signpost and follow the track to the immediate left of the bungalow. Continue on into the field beyond. The track soon bends to the left. Ignore any tracks to the right, and continue along the edge of the field. Eventually, the road is reached as the path goes alongside the edge of a house.

Go right and, as the road rises over the old railway bridge, look for the signpost in the fence on the left, just past a house. Through a gap in the fence, drop down with care into the field below. Go forward with the hedge and then some fencing on the left. Keeping to the right-hand side of the stream, head for the footbridge ahead. Then, follow the wide track ahead, until it reaches the road, by the signpost at the right of the hedge surrounding the house.

2. *Turn right along the road.* Just before the bridge, go through the gate to the left into the large area of the old Barton station. It is possible to see the remains of the platform of the old station. This was on a branch of what used to be the old Aintree to Southport main line and is now the Cheshire Lines cycle and walk track. The Barton spur, which ran into Southport via Shirdley Hill, was opened in 1887. The station closed in 1936 and the line itself in 1952. The Barton Spur is particularly remembered because of the 'Altcar Bob', which was driveable from either end and hence avoided the need of a turn-table.

Since this area is now the Haskayne Nature Reserve, there is no public right of way through it without a permit. So return to the gate by the bridge and turn right along the path, signposted Haskayne, which follows the fence along the edge of the old rail cutting. Where steps come up from the cutting, turn left through the fields along a wide farm track. As the track goes on, turn right along the right side of a stream. Near to the houses, turn left over a footbridge. Continue with the hedge and factory grounds on your right. The path bends to the right, as it goes along the back of a shed and onto the road.

3. *With the factory entrance to the right*, follow the road straight ahead, with the shop on the left. After some bungalows on the left-hand side, turn left along the signposted path opposite to Park Crescent. The way runs between the gardens of houses and the stream. At the end of the path, go left along the narrow lane and by the Kings Head pub, turn sharp right back up the main road towards the canal bridge. Descend to the tow path and walk to the left. Continue to the next road bridge, with the Ship Inn on the left.

Keep on down the tow path and under a second bridge. This is the oldest section of the Liverpool to Leeds canal, for it was in Halsall with easy access to materials, that the work was begun in the eighteenth century.

Thatched cottage at Haskayne

4. *At the end of the cutting is a small bridge*, which for a change does not carry a road. To extend the walk, cross the bridge and continue through the kissing-gate until Bangor's Farm is reached. Coming into the road, turn right immediately along the farm track, with the farm house on the left. The track swings sharply to the right and then arrives at a wooden bridge over a stream. The path then continues to the left along the edge of the stream. As it bends away to the left, go at right angles and walk to reach the lane called Trundle Pie Lane. Here, turn right back towards the canal. As it is reached, turn right, passing the war time pill-box. At the bridge, return to the tow-path and the shorter walk.

Go ahead to the next road bridge, with yet another canal pub, waiting to refresh the weary traveller. Turn left along the road back to Halsall church and the Saracen's Head pub.

Walk 10

Ince Blundell

A walk in the countryside surrounding Ince Blundell near Crosby.

Route: Ince Blundell village — Carr Houses — Baines Bridge — Ince Blundell Park — Ince Blundell village.

Start: Ince Blundell Village. Grid reference: 322 035.

Distance: 3½ miles.

Duration: 1½ hours.

Map: SD20/30.

By train: None.

By car: At the Weld Blundell pub (grid ref. 317 039) turn left off the A565 along the minor road to Ince Blundell (Lady Green Lane). It is possible to park in the next road on the right.

Refreshments: The Weld Blundell.

---

1. *Returning to Lady Green Lane, turn right.* Walk on the far side of the road. Having gone round a sharp bend, turn left at a sign into a farm. Keep to the right of the buildings, with a ditch on the right. After a while, the farm track bears to the left, and as the ditch goes away at right angles, continue across the middle of the field to reach Carr House Lane.

Turn right along the road until Carr Houses are reached. This is a conservation area. Between the buildings on the right, turn into the lane. Pass the barn on the right and continue down the winding road through fields. After passing through an avenue of trees, the road turns sharply to the right.

Keeper's Cottage

2. *Here, follow the footpath signs down the track to the left,* which leads into the grounds of Keeper's Cottage, although it is a bit more than a cottage these days. Going close to the left-hand side of the house, go towards the two wooden posts ahead and on, into the wood. The wide track keeps near to the edge of the wood. As it swings to the right, a field can be seen ahead at the end of the wood.

Instead of going ahead into the field, turn left along the left-hand side of a ditch. As you emerge into a field, continue along the edge of the ditch. At the junction of ditches, do not

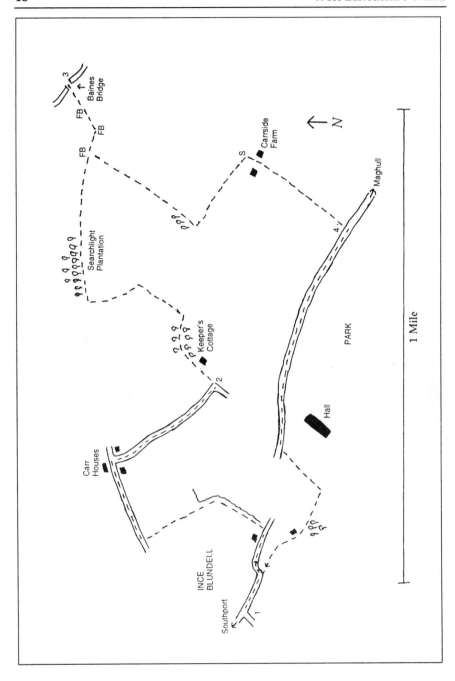

cross the plank of wood that serves as a bridge. Turn left, with a ditch still on the right. When the ditch finishes, keep ahead across the field, towards the left side of Searchlight Plantation, where there is a footpath sign. Turn right along the edge of the wood, in the direction of the sign.

This is a wide track. As the wood ends, go ahead, with a line of poles on the right and soon a ditch to the left. Go over the footbridge by a pole. Keep ahead and turn left over another footbridge. Cross a third bridge to arrive up the steps at Baines Bridge over the River Alt.

Baines Bridge was erected in 1993. The Ramblers' Association had campaigned for it over many years. The previous bridge had been removed in 1891 and so there had been no link between the Lancashire and Merseyside sides of the river for over a century. This had meant it was impossible to link the footpaths in the area. The cost of the new bridge, some £120,000, was shared jointly by Lancashire County Council, Sefton Council and the Countryside Commission.

3. *Now return from the bridge over the two footbridges* and then turn right, back to the third bridge. Do not cross it this time, but turn left towards the wood in the distance. As the edge of the wood is reached, cross two stiles in fenced off parts of the larger field. At the corner of the second fenced field, almost at the extremity of the wood on the right, turn left along the edge of a stream. The field is likely to contain a number of large white Charolais cattle, which might, at first sight, be taken for bulls. They are very docile and will not take much notice of your passage.

At the end of the field, there is a stile, with a signpost pointing back to Baines Bridge and Lydiate. Turn right, passing the imposing house of Carrside Farm on the right, and proceed down the lane, towards the road. Looking over to the right, it is possible to see Ince Blundell Hall, set in the midst of parkland. The Blundell family were the lords of the manor from the twelfth century, but in the nineteenth century the Weld family took control. The present hall was built in 1729. Ince Blundell, along with Little Crosby, was historically a strong centre of Catholicism. Although the hall itself is now a retirement home, the Roman Catholic chapel still remains in operation.

4. *On reaching the road, it is possible to see through the open gateway* into the parkland, but a large notice is a reminder that the area is private property. Turn right along Park Wall Road. The wall itself was built in the 1770s. Look for the white cross painted on it at one point. This was originally the site of the ancient wayside cross, which was moved into the grounds of the Hall in the eighteenth century. The wall ends at the entrance to the Hall and the Chapel. After walking by a green mesh fence in front of trees, turn left into a track, known as Cross Barn Lane.

Next, turn right at the signpost. The path runs between a field and then a wood on the left and a broken fence on the right. Away to the right a cemetery can be seen. The path narrows as it passes in front of Gable Cottage and then broadens out, with houses on either side. At the end of the lane, you are back at the start of the walk.

Walk 11

Lydiate

A route which includes the old Cheshire Lines Railway and also two historic buildings, Lydiate Hall and St Katherine's Chapel.

Route: Hall Lane – Cheshire Lines – Canal – Hall Lane.

Start: Our Lady's RC Church, Hall Lane Lydiate. Grid reference: 364 052

Distance: 4½ miles.

Duration: 1½ hours.

Map: SD20/30.

By train: None.

By car: Parking in Hall Lane. Travelling in the Southport direction out of Lydiate, this is reached soon after the main housing ends. Turn right off the A567 by the church.

Refreshments: Running Horses, Lydiate.

---

1. *The starting point is Our Lady's RC Church.* This was built in 1854, when the domestic chapel at Lydiate Hall became too small for services. Turn left back along the main road, which fortunately has a pavement on the left-hand side. Just before a tall wall begins on the left, cross the road and follow the signpost into a field. To the right of the signpost is an advert for Lydiate Hall farm. Continue along the right edge of the

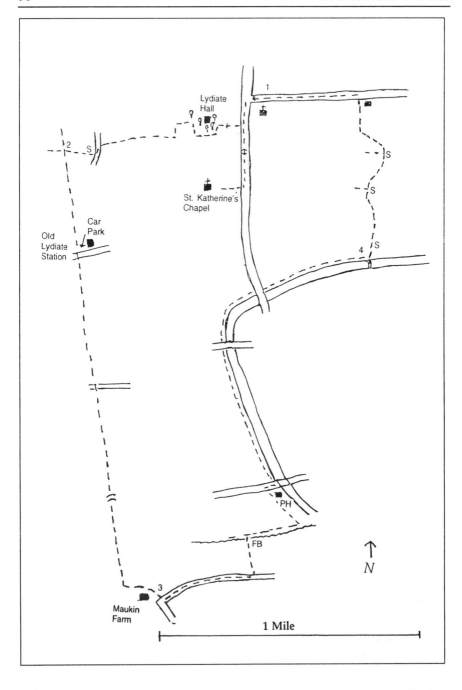

Lydiate
Hall

1

2   S

St. Katherine's
Chapel

S

S

Car
Park

Old
Lydiate
Station

4   S

PH

FB

↑
N

3

Maukin
Farm

1 Mile

field and then bear to the left and right round woodland, following the waymarkers.

Amidst the trees are the ruins of Lydiate Hall. They are on private land, so best viewed during the winter months when the trees have no leaves. The Hall dates back to the century and was owned by the Ireland family originally and most recently by the Blundell family. Over the years it fell into a state of chronic disrepair. The oldest part, the East wing, was destroyed as far back as 1779. It is thought that the stone was used to build the present farm shop.

Over the centuries the Hall was a Catholic stronghold. The Ireland family also built St Katherine's Chapel, the substantial remains of which can be seen across the field to the left. A closer look is obtained by going back along the road, from which access can be gained.

St Katherine's Chapel

Turn right down a farm track in the same field on the third side of the wood. Then turn left at the waymarker and follow the path to the edge of the field. Follow the waymarker to the left and soon turn right at the next marker by a small tree. The path goes to the right of a fence and then continues straight ahead, passing a lone tree and a pond surrounded by trees a little to the left. The path, with a ditch to the left, reaches Acres Lane by a signpost pointing back to Southport Road.

Turn left along the road and, with a signpost on the left side of the road, cross, go over the stile and along the wide track, until reaching a junction, with a copse of small trees on the right.

2. *Turn left and you are now on the Cheshire Lines path*, which provides for walkers, cyclists and horse riders. This is the track bed for the Cheshire Lines railway from Aintree to Southport. In the 1980s, 30 years or so after closure, there was a threat from the local landowner to close access to most of the line. A campaign by local walkers persuaded the local authorities to keep it open. It was then made into a leisure way by Sustrans Ltd.

Continuing down the path, arrive at Carr Lane. This is the site of the old Lydiate station, first opened in 1884 and closed in 1952. The only remains of its existence are the former station cottages. Keep ahead and pass a pond on the left before reaching Cabin Lane. This is the Gore House Conservation Area, looked after by the North West Ecological Trust.

Further along pass under a bridge and continue to the end of the stone pathway, the present end point of the route. It is hoped that in the future this will be extended, as it becomes part of the Trans-Pennine Trail. Turn left along the trackway towards Maukin Farm.

3. *Coming into Green Lane by the farm*, follow the road to the

left. Eventually, just opposite to St James' Church, turn left at the signpost. This will take you down to a stream. Cross the bridge and then turn right along the bank. Then follow the path to the left, until it reaches the road by the Running Horses pub.

From here go left along the canal tow path from the swing bridge, properly called Sumners Turn Bridge. This section of the canal is usually full of brightly coloured boats and barges. On the left is open country, on the right houses. Pass under two road bridges. Just before the first of these, Lydiate Bridge, look for the winding hole on the other side of the canal, into which barges reversed in order to turn round. The second bridge is called Lollies Bridge. Each has seats just before reaching them, if a rest is needed at this stage. The third bridge reached is Lydiate Hill Bridge.

4. *Go up the steps onto the bridge and turn left along the path.* This reaches one stile, and then, continuing between fences, another. It goes along the edge of the field, coming to a stile by a horses' gallop track. Cross the track and over another stile. Go to the right, keeping to the edge of another part of the horse track railings. Then two more stiles across the track and immediately through a gate, turning left along a path, which again stays close to the rails.

The path then goes to the right, bears to the left, alongside some trees, and past a lone tree, as it swings to the right again. There are white topped way markers to help direction finding. The path goes immediately to the left of some trees, and then, down a short wide farm track, onto Hall Lane. Turn left and walk back to the church.

Walk 12

Melling

Never far from the suburbs of Liverpool, this walk meanders through pleasant agricultural countryside and the ancient village of Melling.

Route: Maghull Station – Guest Farm – St Thomas' Church – Maghull Station.

Start: The station, Station Road, Maghull. Grid reference: 384 014.

Distance: 5 miles.

Duration: 2 hours.

Map: SD20/30

By train: Maghull is on the Northern Line of Merseyrail to Ormskirk. Trains in both directions every 15 minutes, except for evenings and Sundays when it is 30 minutes.

By Car. To reach the station car park from the Liverpool direction, turn right off the A59 at Maghull Town Hall (Map ref: 374 015), at the traffic lights. Go down Hall Lane. Continue over the canal bridge and straight on, still on Hall Lane. Then bear right down Station Road, until reaching the station.

Refreshments: Bootle Arms, Melling.

---

1. *Turn left out of the station and walk along Melling Lane,* passing Grange Park and Summerhill Drive. Eventually the

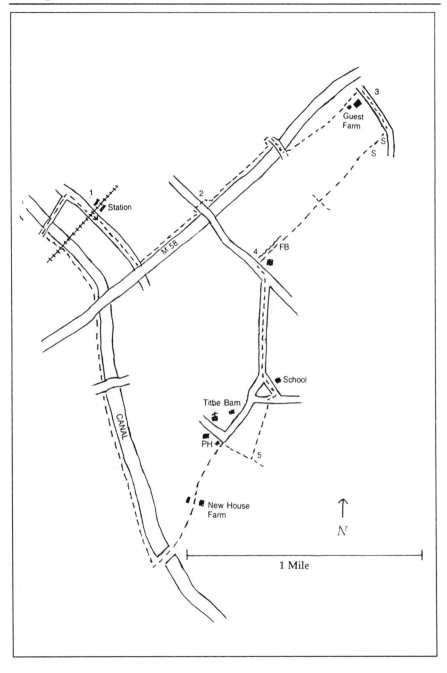

1 Mile

houses come to an end. There is a hedge, beyond which is the playing field. Do not turn left at the first two gaps, but continue on until reaching a sign post, just before the motorway viaduct.

Go left along the edge of the playing field, passing a children's play area. The track then bends to the left, passing through a gate, which is usually left open. Some steps to the left go up to an elevated grass area, where there is a seat. Follow the steps that climb up to the road on the right.

2. *Cross over the road.* A gate, stile, signpost and waymarker indicate the route along a metal road. This runs parallel to the M58, divided from it by a fence. On the left are open fields. As the bridge is approached, the path swings up to the left, where there is a communications tower and a three headed signpost. Go to the right over the bridge and then left, following the signpost indicating Giddygate Lane. The metal road soon becomes a dirt track, which continues close to the motorway, until Guest Farm is reached. Until recently the right of way was to follow the track in front of the farm onto the road. A diversion means that the path now follows a route to the back of the wooden shed, reaching Giddygate Lane almost adjacent to the M58.

3. *Turn right along the narrow lane,* until reaching a house on the right. On the left-hand side of the road is a double signpost by a foot bridge. On the far side of the house, next to the drive, is a stile. Cross this into an area of what seems to be no-man's land. The path is close to the hedge on the right. Continue, over another stile, into a field. The path stays on the left side of the ditch, following a line of telegraph poles. Then over a plank over a ditch into another field. Eventually, cross over a farm track, with a house to your right and go on following the waymarker ahead. There is now a high hedge to the right.

At the end of this field, go over the bridge, along the well-worn path, which goes between the ditch and trees on the right and the waterworks on the left. This emerges on Leatherbarrows Lane.

4. *Turn left along the road and almost immediately right into Sandy Lane.* Along this narrow road, turn left into School Lane. On the left is Melling School, which was founded in 1844.

At the end of the short School Lane, almost immediately opposite across Tithebarn Lane, is a bus-shelter. To the right of the shelter is a footpath sign of some size. Follow the wide track between it and the high wall of the house. This follows the poles out into open fields, after the long wall and a fence on the right. Looking across to the right, the buildings along Tithebarn Lane can be seen. Note the fine stone edifice of the old vicarage, built in 1831. On its left is the ancient Tithebarn, hidden in the trees. Here, the tithes were brought in belonging to the Rector of Halsall. In years gone by Melling, Maghull and Lydiate were all part of the parish of Halsall. Even today the Rector of Halsall still has a share in the patronage (i.e. appointing the vicar) of the now individual parishes. After some years as the coach-house of the vicarage last century, today the Tithebarn is both a parish hall and also a centre for recitals and concerts.

5. *On reaching the end of the field,* turn right along the track that runs along the far side of the hedge, not any that are on the near side. When the track reaches the road, the route is to the left, but pause if you want refreshments and a look at the parish church. These are a few metres ahead along Rock Lane. On the left is the Bootle Arms and on the right St Thomas' Church. Although the church only dates back to 1834, it is on the site of the Chapel of the Holy Cross, dating from 1190. The fact that there are gravestones which are even older, indicates Christian worship here for well over 1,000 years.

Return now back down the road, to the point where Tithebarn Lane goes to the left. Turn right by the house on the corner, and go down the narrow hedged lane. Go through New House Farm and follow the track to Holmes swingbridge. Turn right along the tow path. This part of the canal was built in 1771.

6. *The next bridge is Melling Stone Bridge.* Just before it, two winding holes are to be seen on the other side of the canal. It was here that, having picked up stone from Melling Quarry, the barges turned round. Continue, passing under the M58 and the railway bridge, until reaching Drapers Bridge. Cross and continue up Rutherford Road. Then turn right back to the station.

The Bootle Arms

Walk 13

Martin Mere

A pleasant walk around the land that used to be covered by the Mere, which can be complemented by a visit to the Wildfowl Centre. Please note: it is of great help to Martin Mere Wildfowl and Wetlands Trust if this route is not used between October and March.

Route: Martin Mere – Canal – Burscough Village – Martin Mere.

Start: Martin Mere Wildfowl Trust car park. Grid reference: 430 144.

Distance: 5 or 4½ miles.

Duration: 2 or 1½ hours.,

Map: SD41/51.

By train: None.

By car: The car park at Martin Mere is reached by following the road to the left, immediately after crossing the station bridge in Burscough on the A59.

Refreshments: A number of cafes and pubs in Burscough and a cafe at Martin Mere if you pay to go into the Wildfowl Trust. Martin Mere Wildfowl and Wetlands Trust is open daily from 9.30am – 5.30pm in summer, 4.00pm in winter. Closed 24th and 25th of December.

---

1. *From the car park, turn right along the road.* Ignore the track over the footbridge on the right. Look for a wide cart track on the right.

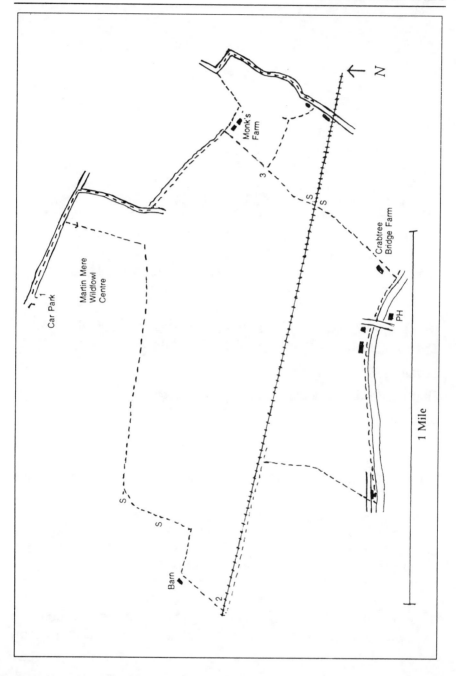

Then turn right along the cart track, alongside the perimeter fence of the Wildfowl Trust. At the end of the fence, follow the track at right angles, with the fence to the right and a stream on the left. As the perimeter fence ends, go straight ahead across, first of all, a wooden bridge and then one with a concrete base. The track continues on, with the stream on the left. Look for a stile on the left, beside a gate. Go along the edge of the field, close to the fence. Then over another stile into another field. Then turn right, aiming towards an old barn along a farm track. There is a stream on the left-hand side. At the barn go left, until reaching the railway.

2. *Across the railway, turn left.* The path runs along the railway fence for a good distance. When eventually the sewage works can be seen on the opposite side of the railway, look for the track that goes to the right. Do not go straight to New Lane station, which can be seen ahead. The track to the right is another long one through open fields. Do not take any of the turns off, but keeping going until reaching Gorst Lane.

Cross the road and go up the short lane, next to the saw mill, onto the canal tow path. Do not cross the Great Score swing bridge, but turn left down the tow path. After passing some of the old canal workers cottages, arrive at the Crabtree swing bridge. Proceed on and soon turn left down the track to Crabtree Bridge Farm. Passing the barn which is on the right, the track goes straight ahead, passing the garden hedge of the farmhouse. Go on through the middle of the field. Cross the bridge across the stream and continue ahead to the railway crossing. Go over the stiles on either side of the rails. Follow the clear track ahead. After the third lone tree, there is a choice of ways.

3. *The shorter route is to cross the field ahead,* aiming for the barn at the left-hand side of the cluster of buildings. The longer way is to turn right at the third tree, passing another tree to

reach a track from the left. Turn right and follow the track between hedges, until it reaches a road. Here, turn left. The road turns sharply to the left and then to the right. At this second bend, turn left up the concrete drive, with a hedge to the left. On reaching the two gate pillars of the house at the end of the drive, turn right and follow the path round to the barn to the right of the large house. The shorter route is joined at the barn.

From the barn, the path is on the left-hand side of the stream. After a while, it reaches a road on a sharp corner. Turn to the right and follow the road until it reaches a T-Junction. Here, turn left back to Martin Mere.

Martin Mere (by kind permission of Dr Janet Kear, Martin Mere)

Walk 14

Mawdesley

A popular walk, taking in the local beauty spot, Harrock Hill. Much of the route is flat, but there is a steady ascent to the hill itself.

Route: Hurst Green – Cedar Farm – Harrock Hill – Andertons Mill – Hurst Green.

Start: Village Hall car park, off Hurst Green Mawdesley. Grid reference: 493 150

Distance: 4½ miles.

Duration: 3 hours.

Map: SD41/51.

By train: None.

By car: Mawdesley is most easily approached by taking the B5246 road towards Parbold from the A59 at Rufford. After approximately 1 mile take the left turn to Mawdesley. At the cross roads in the centre of the village turn left and then left into Hurst Green just past the Red Lion. Turn right, beyond the school into the car park.

Refreshments: Red Lion and Cedar Farm.

---

1. *From the car park, walk back along Hurst Green to New Street.* Turn right, passing the Red Lion, to the cross roads. Keep straight on, with the Methodist church on the left. Then over

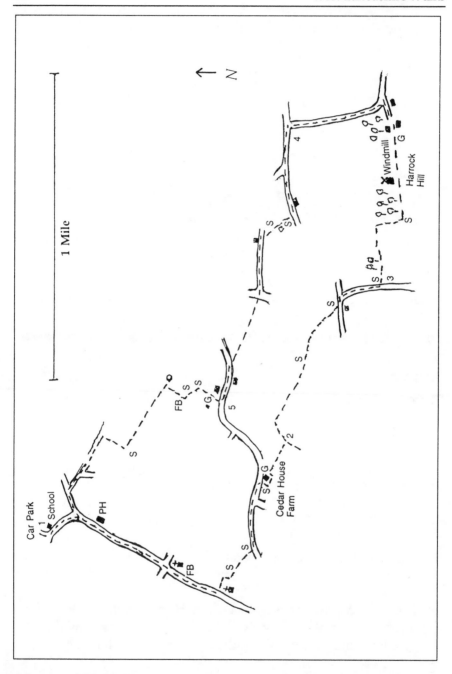

a footbridge, continuing until just before St Peter's Parish Church. Go left at the signpost, squeezing between upright poles. The path proceeds, with a fence to the left and the hedge of the graveyard to the right. It swings at right angles, until it reaches another set of 'squeeze between' poles.

Go towards the right-hand corner of the field, just a short distance ahead. Over the double stile, stay on the right. In a few metres, you will be able to see the next stile, by a gate, towards the left-hand side of the opposite side of the field.

You are now in School Lane. Walking to the left, turn left again at the road junction, until Cedar House Farm is reached. This is a craft and exhibition centre, open to the public every day, except Mondays, from 10.00am – 5.00pm. Refreshments are available. The stile, by the signpost, leads into the car park. The path is straight ahead, although it tends to be obscured from sight by a large fir tree. Go between that tree and the animal pen on the right and proceed, with trees to the left and a fence to the right. Over the stile, turn left along the back of some wooden sheds and left at the end of them. There is another stile, although the gate is usually open. Walk along the wide farm track to the right.

2. *At the junction, turn left.* Opposite to a copse of trees on the left, turn right over a stile at the corner of the fencing. Keeping the fence to the left, continue until the stream is on your left. Cross a stile and plank over a ditch and walk on until reaching the road, over a stile. Turn left and almost immediately right, opposite a house, into Jackson's Lane.

The road begins to rise gradually. Passing two splendid houses opposite to each other, soon look for a signpost and double stile on the left. Keep to the left-hand edge of the field and then over a stile in the fencing, into a woodland glade. Continue up through the avenue of trees, over another stile, until it looks as if the way ahead is blocked by a fence. On the right, squeezed between a tree and the fence, is a stile.

3. *Over the stile, go uphill, with the fence on the left,* over a second stile, until the left-hand corner of the field is reached. Now, go right, still upwards, along the side of the wood. There are fine views over Mawdesley and beyond, looking back from here.

At the top of the field, turn left along a path that runs between a stone wall and the trees. At the end of this, just ahead, is the old ruined windmill. It is possible to see the track along which the grain was brought into the basement of the mill for grinding. Imagine what an effort it must have been for horses to drag the loads up the hill. This is the summit of Harrock Hill and a good place to pause to admire the extensive views.

The ruined windmill on Harrock Hill

Carry on along the brow of the hill and then start to descend down the stone track. This leads through a gap by a gate, through the farmyard and down a pot-holed road. Turn left at the road junction, by the house on the right. On turning to the left, there is a seat on the right. From here, there is a good view across towards the M6 and Camelot, the leisure park. The road now descends rapidly for about half a mile, eventually with houses on either side.

4. *At the junction, turn left onto a busier road.* This is the Andertons Mill area. Pass the road that goes to the right and continue straight on. Keep on, passing the farm to the right, and then, after a bungalow on the left, there is a sign and stile on the right-hand side of the road. Follow the edge of the field, skirting to the right of the pond and then back to the stile in the fence. Then follow the hedge, until reaching the road, opposite a house.

Walk along the road to the left until a junction is reached. Immediately opposite is a wide track, which leads towards a high hedge in the distance. The path narrows, as it continues to the left of the hedge, until it reaches the road by a field gate. Turn left and pass a house on the left, until coming to one on the right, set back from the road.

5. *Immediately after the house is a stile,* with a signpost marked 'Bradshaw Brow'. Walk, with the hedge to the right, through a double gate. Then past a large barn on the left and through another gate. The path continues to follow the edge of the field, swinging to the left and through two stiles. Soon after the second stile, the path veers sharply right to the stream and a footbridge. Keep to the left of the hedge in the next field, until it reaches a pond in the right corner. Bear left, passing a hedge on the left, until reaching a stile.

Over the stile, turn right. There is a housing estate on the left. Keep by the hedge, until reaching a footbridge over the stream. Do not cross, but follow the pathway on the left, between the stream and the houses. This leads onto an estate road. Go ahead and soon turn right into Tarnbeck Drive. This takes you down to New Street. Turn left and then right into Hurst Green and back to the car park.

Walk 15

Ormskirk (1)

Never far away from the town of Ormskirk, the walk touches on Lathom and Westhead. Except for one short section, it is entirely through open country. The only modest uphill stretch is towards the end.

Route: Ruff Wood – Lathom – Westhead Village – Ruff Wood.

Start: Ruff Wood, Ormskirk. Grid reference: 074 428

Distance: 6 miles.

Duration: 3 hours.

Map: SD40/50 and SD41/51

By train: Ormskirk station is the terminus for the Merseyrail service from Liverpool as well as trains from Preston. The start of the walk is reached by walking to the town centre and then along Knowsley Road, Ruff Lane and Vicarage Lane.

By car: Car parking by the wood in Vicarage Lane, just off Ruff Lane.

Refreshments: Halton Castle pub in Westhead village.

---

1. *The wood is properly known as the Ruff.* By the Ruff Lane entrance is placed a plaque which states that the wood was given to the public in 1912 by Thomas Holcroft. In earlier times it was known as 'The Roughs', because of the up and down nature of the terrain, mainly caused by quarry workings.

Just as Vicarage Lane turns sharply to the right by the corner of the wood, follow the signpost into the wood itself. Keep to the path to the right, with the house on that side. Continue around the edge of the wood, ignoring paths to the left. At a wood gate, turn right away from the wood and along the track across the middle of the field. Ormskirk Hospital is in the distance to the left.

2. *Reaching Crosshall Brow, turn right* and then immediately left by the signpost. Go down the side track which leads by a house and barns. Notice that the ancient barn on the left is dated 1681.

Continue on the track down hill. On the left is a Gas Board Installation and on the right a path along the old railway embankment. This was the line from Ormskirk to Skelmersdale, know locally as the 'Jazzer'.

The track ahead eventually crosses over a small stream and then a wood to the right, arriving at Lathom Lane. The path ahead is not a right of way, although many walkers use it. Turn right to the cross roads and then to the left along Sandy Lane. On the right, after a few hundred metres, is a public footpath sign. It is on the entrance to the house on the right, but after a few metres the path goes straight ahead, crossing a stream. Do not go to the left, but go forward, with the path following the line of telegraph poles. Ignore a well-used path which crosses it. Keep ahead and eventually, at the end of the open fields, a hedge and then a line of trees is on the left.

3. *Turn to the right down a hard track* coming in from the left from the direction of Blythe Hall. This is Lady Alice's Drive, so named because on November 23rd, 1897 somewhere along it, Lady Alice, wife of the first Earl of Lathom, was killed in

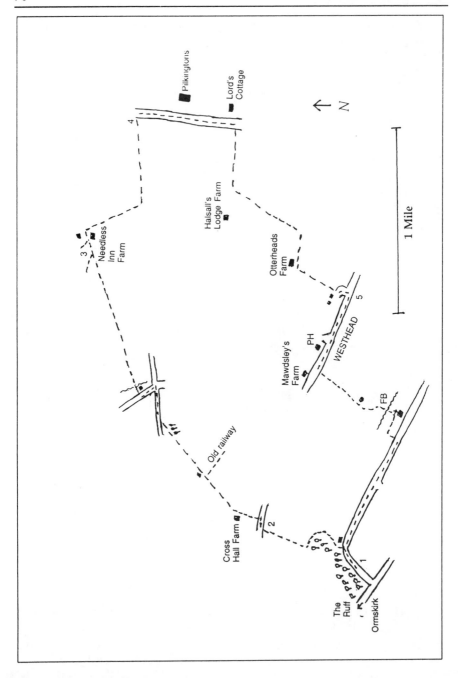

an accident. The story goes that, as she was returning from the hunt, her pony and trap overturned and she was thrown from it.

Following the track to the right, it is joined by another one coming in from the left, and then, by Needless Inn Farmhouse, it turns to the right. The track joins Crane's Lane at a junction. Here, turn left and follow it until it reaches the road. Lathom Park is opposite. If it is not to be visited on Walk No.16, then now is an opportunity to do so. Please refer to that walk for details.

4. *Turn right along the road*, passing the Lathom base of Pilkington's Glass to the left. The building would not win too many prizes for architectural merit, standing as it does in the middle of open countryside. A little further on, turn right by a signpost opposite to Lord's Cottage. The farm track leads towards Halsall's Lodge Farm. Before reaching it, turn left by the signpost on a telegraph pole. The track eventually peters out. The way is now on the line of the telegraph poles straight ahead.

Arriving at a wide track, turn right and follow it as it bends to the left by Otterheads Farm. Going by a pond on the right, the track emerges in Greenacres, a small housing estate. From here go the few metres to the main road.

5. *Cross the road and continue to the right,* passing the Halton Castle pub and Castle Lane to the right. Opposite Mawdsley's Farm shop, turn left between the houses. There is a public footpath sign. The track, with trees planted along the left-hand side, starts to go uphill. Passing a farm building to the right, the path goes ahead, as the track bends towards the house on the left. The path passes to the right of the house and, after going along a hedge, turns to the left. Then it goes fairly steeply downhill to the stream. Across the footbridge, it climbs again and follows round the wall of the churchyard to arrive at the

road. A few metres to the left is the ancient Lych gate, where coffins were rested.

6. *Go right along the road, passing Wellfield Lane,* St James' Close and Vicarage Close, back to Ruff Wood and the car.

The ancient lych gate at St James' Church, Westhead

Walk 16

Ormskirk (2)

Monks, musicals and muskets feature in this walk.
Burscough Priory, Blythe Hall and Lathom Park are all
steeped in history and associations with the past.

Route: Lathom Park – Blythe Hall – Burscough Priory – Lathom Park.

Start: Lay-by at Lathom Park Chapel on B5240. Grid reference: 455 092

Distance: 5 miles.

Duration: 2 hours.

Map: SD40/50 and 41/51.

By train: None.

By car: Turn right about half a mile outside Burscough (A5209 to Parbold) just beyond the Briars Hall Hotel.

Refreshments: None.

1. *Cross the road onto the wide signposted track of Crane Lane* opposite. Continue for some distance, ignoring the track to the right. Having passed through the car park of Ormskirk golf club and Robinson's Farm, arrive at the cross roads. Turn right into Sandy Lane. Do not take the path to the right by the house on the corner. Go on down Sandy Lane, turning right at the next footpath sign, by the drive to a house. For the first few

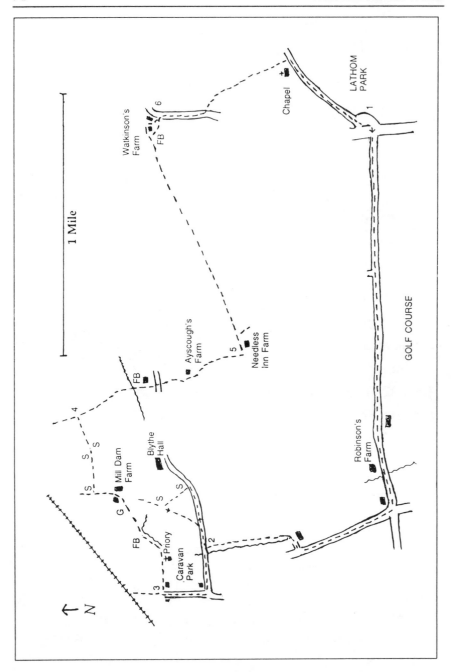

metres the path is on the drive, but as this bends to the right, go straight ahead over the stream.

Turn left and stay close to the bank of the stream, until reaching the road by the bridge. This is Blythe Lane.

2. *Turn right along the road.* Pass one footpath sign just before the corner and then, just round the sharp bend, go left over a stile into a field. Cross towards a stile in the distance in the opposite hedge. It is difficult to see until getting close to it. From this field, there are good views of Blythe Hall.

There has been a hall on the site since the twelfth century. In 1826, it was purchased by Edward Bootle-Wilbraham, who lived in Lathom House. He was later to become the second Lord Skelmersdale. Then, in 1880, he was made the first Earl of Lathom. In 1922, the third Earl decided to come to live in Blythe Hall, since Lathom House was full of dry rot. He extended the Hall considerably, adding a new wing to it. The Earl was a great man of the theatre. Many friends were entertained at the Hall, including Ivor Novello, Noel Coward and Gladys Cooper. Unfortunately, the Earl died at the age of 35 in 1930 without an heir. The Hall is now a private residence.

Over the stile, turn left along the wide track, which will bring you back to the road and Abbey bridge, where you were before the Blythe Hall detour. Turn left along the road. Where the road swings sharply to the left, go right by the house on the corner. There is a signpost, plus a notice indicating Abbey Farm Caravan site. The private road notice does not apply to walkers. Carry on down the metal road, passing the car park on the left and caravans on the right.

3. *Ahead, between a barn and farmhouse,* is a gate. Do not follow the track that swings right immediately before the gate, but go through the gap to the left of the gate. Do not follow the track

ahead towards the railway. Rather, turn right, keeping to the
edge of the field. Just after the farmhouse on the right, it is
possible to glimpse the few remains of Burscough Priory
through gaps in the hedge. The Priory was founded in 1189
by the Augustine order. At the time it was dissolved in 1536,
it was staffed by a prior and four canons. The rood screen,
lectern and font are now housed in Lathom Park Chapel. The
bells were removed to Ormskirk Parish Church. A tower,
probably of stones from the Priory, was built to house them.
Hence Ormskirk Parish Church is one of the few to have both
a spire and a tower.

At the corner of the field, turn left along the bank of the stream.
Then cross a footbridge and stile. Stay on the edge of the field,
as the stream veers away to the right. Go through the gate by
the barn, then turn left up the stone track leading away from
Mill Dam Farm. Next turn right, by the sign over the metal
stile. Walk along the left-hand side of the remains of a fence.
At the next stile, go the short distance through the trees to
another stile. Then aim across the wide field towards a stile
in a wire fence.

4. *Turn right down the fenced wide farm track.* As this goes to the
   left, carry on ahead down the narrow path to a concrete
   footbridge. Follow the path uphill, first with a fence and then
   a brick wall to the right. Coming out by the houses to the left,
   continue on down the drive to the road. Cross directly over
   the road onto a farm track by a footpath sign. The track passes
   through Ayscough's Farm, with Jumps Barn on the left. Proceed on, as the track goes through open fields.

5. *At Needless Inn Farm,* do not follow the main route around to
   the right, but continue straight on along another track. This
   has a line of telegraph poles along the right-hand side of it.

The wide track narrows, as it goes on the right-hand side of
the hedge. The poles are now on the left side. Over to the right

is Alice's Plantation. As the hedge comes to an end, do not follow the track to the left. Keep ahead, staying on the right-hand side of the ditch. You soon come onto a wider path leading towards Watkinson's Farm, which can be seen in the distance. The official right of way goes to the right along the near edge of the stream just before the barn. At a lone tree cross the footbridge and walk across the field to meet the farm track just to the right of the farm house. From there, proceed the few metres to the road. The present owners of the farm are happy for walkers to follow the main track all the way through the farm rather than follow the official right of way round the back.

6. *At the road, go right along the pavement.* On reaching the war memorial on the opposite side of the road, follow the lane to the left of it, marked 'Private road to Parklands. Footpath only to Lathom Park Chapel'. Keep on the path until it reaches the chapel and it's almshouses. The chapel dates from 1500, when

Lathom Park chapel

it was built as a chapel of ease by the first Lord Derby. It is all that remains of the original estate and is now part of the parish of Ormskirk. This beautiful little place of worship contains some of the furnishings from Burscough Priory previously mentioned. The screen has some bullet holes in it, apparently a legacy of the Parliamentary siege. The organ is notable for having black naturals and white sharps on the keyboard. In the grounds is a stone from which the Parliamentary forces are said to have taken material for cannon balls.

From the front entrance to the chapel, it is possible to see the west wing of the second Lathom House across the park. This is all that remains after the demolition in 1920. The original house is believed to have stood a little to the south-east in Spa Roughs. It was a fortified manor house completely demolished during the Civil War. The house was under siege for 88 days in 1642, being defended by Countess Charlotte de Tremouille and 300 troops against vastly superior forces. But, in the following year, the Parliamentary forces under General Egerton eventually overran the defenders, in spite of heroic resistance. The track to Lathom House is private.

Turn right from the chapel entrance and arrive back at the starting point.

Walk 17

Ormskirk (3)

Clieves (Clive's) Hill is a beautiful area of rising ground on the outskirts of Ormskirk. A couple of minutes after leaving the busy Liverpool to Preston Road, the walker is out in the countryside and well away from it all.

Route: St Anne's Road, Ormskirk – Devil's Wall – Clieves Hill – St Anne's Road.

Start: St Anne's Road, Ormskirk. Grid reference: 409 078.

Distance: 4½ or 2½ miles.

Duration: 2½ or 1½ hours.

Map: SD20/30 and SD40/50.

By train: Ormskirk station is the terminus for the Merseyrail service from Liverpool as well as trains from Preston. The start of the walk is reached by walking to the town centre and then down Aughton Street to the A59 roundabout.

By car: St Anne's Road is adjacent to the A59 roundabout that links County Road and Holborn Hill.

Refreshments: None on the actual walk. A variety of choice in Ormskirk.

---

1. *Walk back to the main road turning left towards Liverpool.* Cross this busy road with care. After a hundred metres or so, look for a wide opening between the houses, marked by a sign

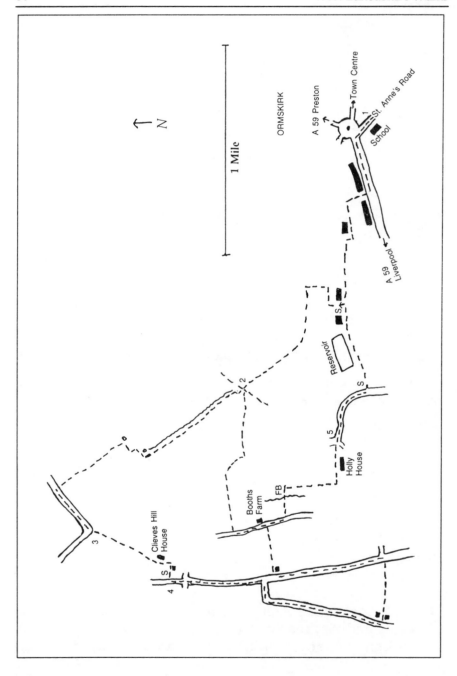

post. Follow the well-defined track, which soon swings to the left. Passing the farm on the right, proceed up the hill.

As the hill levels out, the main path continues on. Immediately past the large shed, turn right. The path is between the high wire fence to the left and a lower one on the right. Follow it round to the right, sharp left and, a little later left again. Eventually, for a short section, the track becomes a sunken one, with a hedge to the left and a high bank to the right. This soon narrows and comes to higher ground.

2. *Coming to the junction of paths, you are now on Devil's Wall,* with fine views towards Halsall and Southport. For the short walk, take a path going downhill towards the left through the gorse. This goes straight on through a field, turns at right angles, and then left along a farm track to Booths Lane. Turn left along the road and meet up with the longer walk at Booths Farm, which is the first building on the left.

The long walk goes ahead at the junction of paths on Devil's Wall. It then bears to the right through the gorse. At the bottom of the slope, follow the path along the edge of a stream. At a group of trees surrounding a pond bear right and then left along a grass track. This soon turns at right angles and continues until it joints the end of the farm track by another group of trees. Turn left onto the track and follow it until it reaches a road. Turn left along the road, until it turns sharply to the right.

3. *Here, go straight ahead at the signpost towards Clieves Hill House,* on rising ground in the distance. Keep to the left of the line of telegraph poles. As the poles go away to the left, continue straight ahead towards the right-hand edge of the wall of the house. The path now follows the right-hand side of the house along a wide grassy verge. At a gate, go over the stile and follow the wide path between the houses. Go through another gate and on to the road.

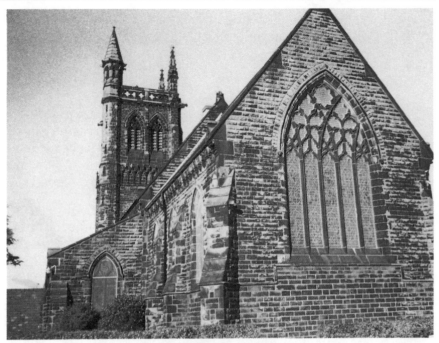

Christ Church, Aughton

4. *Turn left along the road and straight ahead at the crossroads.*
Then go right into Clieves Hill Lane, opposite to a farm. Follow
the road round to the left until the viewpoint is reached, where
there is a seat. From here the road goes downhill. After passing
a number of houses, look for the signposted track on the left.
This has a sharp uphill pull to the immediate left of the
cottages set back from the road. The path continues as a farm
track over open fields, until it reaches the road. Go left along
the road. After a quarter of a mile, turn right along a signposted
path, immediately to the left of a house.

At the end of the first field, look ahead to Booth's Farm in the
distance. Aim for the clump of trees in front of the farm. The
indistinct path is a little to the right of the line of telegraph
poles. On reaching the trees, go to the left of them onto the
road. Turn right and, a little further on, to the left at a sign

post. This takes you along a path which descends gently to a footbridge over a stream. After the bridge go on for a little and then right along a farm track. Follow this track as it goes to the left, alongside the grounds of Holly House nursing home.

5. *Arriving at the road, follow it as it bends to the right.* Look for some steps on the left, which lead to stile. Continue ahead uphill, with the fence on the left, until another stile is reached. Then go along the tarmac path and over another stile. Continue ahead and then downhill on the path, which served the opening part of your journey.

Walk 18

Parbold

An undulating walk, which takes in the famous landmark of Parbold Hill. It gives a good introduction to one of the beauty spots of West Lancashire. The ascent from the level of the canal is very gentle and the lovely view makes the effort well worthwhile.

Route: Parbold Station – Fairy Glen – Parbold Hill – Douglas Chapel – Parbold Station.

Start: Parbold railway station. Grid reference: 492 107.

Distance: 5½ miles.

Duration: 2½ hours.

Map: SD41/51.

By train: Parbold station is on the Southport-Manchester line.

By car: Cars can be parked by the station or by the shopping complex. Coming from Burscough, on the A5209, turn left into Parbold village, over the canal bridge and to the station.

Refreshments: None on the walk.

---

1. *Walk from the station back along the road across the canal bridge.* On the right-hand side of the road is the windmill. This was built in the eighteenth century to replace an earlier one on the River Douglas. This one was superseded about 1850 by

a steam powered corn mill, now demolished, on the north bank. Turn left onto the tow path. After the houses on the far bank, notice the restored dry dock, which marks the starting place of the first route planned for the canal, through Leyland to Skipton rather than Burnley and Blackburn.

Continue along the path, passing under two bridges. Over on the left, the heights of Parbold Hill can be seen, with the

Parbold windmill

church a prominent landmark. At the third bridge turn left and follow the stone track, crossing the railway bridge. Soon another track is met, crossing at right angles.

2. *Turn right and follow the track*, with a cottage standing back from the path on the left. The path then crosses a small paved area, belonging to the house immediately on the left. Go forward on the gravel path for a few metres and then right down a grass path to a stile. If you hear any dogs barking at this stage, they are well caged.

Over the stile, the path drops down through a wooded area to a stream. It then keeps to the fence on the left, as it rises sharply until reaching a stile at a high wooden fence. This is

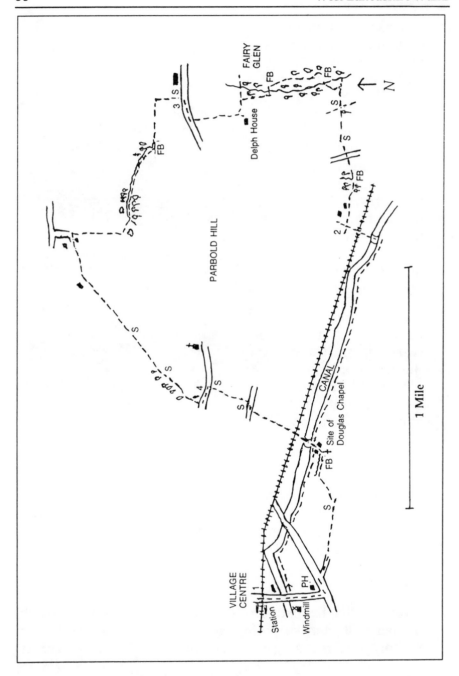

an attempt to shield from view a road constructed to carry waste for the infilling of the huge quarry. Hopefully both fence and road will be removed when the task is completed.

Cross the road. Then, aided by the notice saying 'footpath', go along between the fenced way opposite to the left of the trees. At the end of this, continue straight ahead, going over the stile by a gate. The way ahead is not round the right edge of the field, as some seem to think. The right of way goes straight ahead over the brow of the hill. Aim for the stile to the left of the lone tree ahead. Over the stile, cross a track and find another stile, looking rather lonely, since there is no hedge or fence by it.

Now go straight ahead across the big field towards the woodland in the distance. It is only when you get here, you will see a stile in the railings. Do not go over this, but the one a few metres to the left. This gives a much easier descent into Fairy Glen, an attractive wooded glade. Follow the path down by the railings, towards the bridge that crosses over the stream. Then up the steep steps and turn left along the track, with the stream now on the left. Next, go left across the footbridge and right up the staggered stepway. Back by the stream, ignore the footbridge on the right and continue along the path. When it bears right, take the stile on the left and ascend up the steps to the metal farm road. Turning right, the main road is reached. Cross the road and go right for a short while, until reaching a lay-by.

3. *Just towards the end of the lay-by,* go left by the stone stile and signpost. Go straight ahead, with the hedge to the right. Turn left at the next signpost, along the edge of the field, parallel to the road. Proceed over the stone stile and stream into a glade. The path goes through the trees, bearing right and then left. Now follow it along the edge of the stream. There is a fence on the left. Then cross two stiles, close to each other. After the line of trees on the right-hand side come to an end, there is

plantation on the left. Just after a lone bush on the right of the path, turn right to cross the stream. Go to the right of the pond and pick up a track, going to the right between hedges.

Follow the track until it reaches a junction, with a house on the left. Turn left up the wide track. This then swings sharply left, by the drive of another house. The track continues gently downhill for a good distance. There are excellent views from this section of the walk. At the end of the track, a stile by a gate is reached. Now aim for the corner of the wood on the opposite side of the field. Then follow the edge of the wood over two stiles, the second of which leads into a wooded area. The path dips downwards and then sharply up to the main road.

4. *Cross the road and follow the pavement uphill.* Before reaching the church, turn right over a stile. Keep to the edge of the field as the path descends, until reaching another stile in the right-hand corner of the field. Turn right along the lane and then left. Follow the lane over the railway crossing and arrive at the canal bridge. Walk straight on through the buildings. Just past them, there is a cross in an open space on the left-hand side. This is the site of the old Douglas Chapel. Founded by the Knights Hospitallers of St John, the chapel was erected around 1420. Enlarged over the centuries, it was finally demolished in 1878. Some of the chapel furniture, including the pulpit, was transferred to the new church on the main road ascending Parbold Hill. The old school building, adjoining the present church, was built with stone from the chapel.

Proceeding on, soon to the right, there is a stile. From here the path crosses a stream by means of a bridge and continues along the stream edge. It comes out into a field. Keep to the left, until reaching a stile on the far side of the field. Turn right down the lane until arriving at the main road. Turn left, then right by the pub, back into the centre of Parbold.

Walk 19

Rainford

Railways predominate in this easy walk in the countryside immediately around the village of Rainford.

Route: Siding Lane – Nursery Plantation – Red Delph Farm – Siding Lane.

Start: Siding Lane, Rainford.

Distance: 4 or 2½ miles.

Duration: 2 or 1 hours.

Map: SD40/50

By train: Rainford Junction, if the walk is picked up at point 5.

By car: Siding Lane is reached by turning to the left off the by-pass a mile north west of Rainford, immediately to the north of the railway bridge (Grid reference: 467 023). Drive down Siding Lane to the end of the metal road, passing the old railway cottages on the left. Go into the car park on the left, opposite Franklin's engineering works.

Refreshments: The Golden Lion in the centre of Rainford.

---

1. *Turn left out of the car park and walk along the main path,* passing a number of 'sleeping policemen'. On the left are the overgrown old railway sidings, recalling a time when this was a busy railway depot. With a house on the right, go forward at the signpost. Continue ahead at a waymarked fence, with

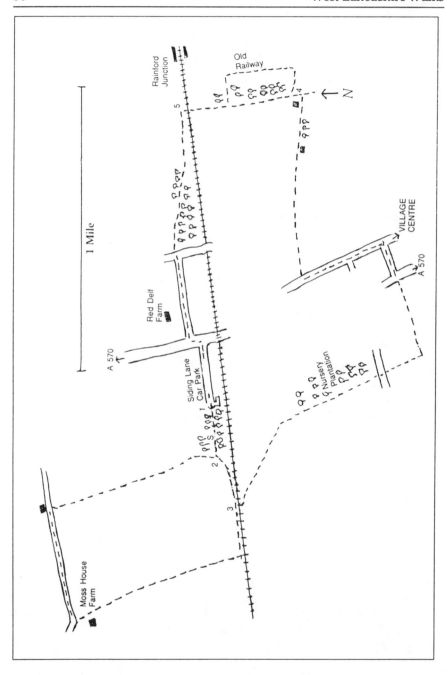

small car park on the right. Pass a pond on the left and arrive at a T-Junction of paths with a double signpost.

2. *Here, the long and short walks divide.* For the longer walk, turn right and, passing a wooden seat on the right, follow the path through the wooded area. Emerging from the wood, the way goes to the right of the two small trees. Aim for the lone big tree straight ahead and continue on until the road is reached. Here, turn left and walk along the road until it swings to the right.

On the bend, go left down the entrance road to Moss House Farm. Continue through the farm buildings, along a wide farm track towards the railway embankment. Having reached it, turn left and keep to the edge of the embankment. After a while, look for a narrow path which brings you onto the wooden crossing of the railway. You now rejoining the route of the shorter walk.

For the shorter walk, turn left at the double signpost. Pass gas marker post 348 on the right. Do not take the first wide track to the left up onto the railway, but the second narrower one soon after. The railway is crossed by means of the wooden sleepers.

3. *Here, the shorter and longer routes join.* Please observe the warning notices. This part of the rail network is in regular use.

From the railway descend the wooden steps. A signpost points the way to a long broad track towards the distant Nursery Plantation. Keeping the trees on the left and ignoring all turns to the left, arrive at a concrete road, which was used for military purposes during the last war. Go straight ahead, by a signpost, along a track across a field and as far as a tree in the second field. Turn left down a wide track to the dual-carriageway. Go straight across and down a small road, until a T-Junction is reached.

At the T-Junction, cross the road and walk to the left. This is the main road out of Rainford (B5203). Walk on past a garage and into open country. Look for a signpost on the right. The path runs between two fences at first and then with just a fence to the left. This meets another track coming in from the left. Go to the right and follow the track around by a house on the right and one on the left. At a T-Junction of paths, with a three pronged signpost, turn left.

4. *There is a choice of routes here.* The shortest is to keep straight ahead, following the path which skirts the woodland on the right, with open fields to the left. Slightly longer is to take the signpost to the right. The path takes you up onto the embank-ment of the old Rainford to St Helens railway. On reaching the bed of the old track, turn left and walk down the wide grassy track. Before reaching the wide length of railings ahead, turn left down a path which links up with the shorter route.

The Golden Lion, Rainford

This area has been landscaped by the local authority as a linear park.

The path along the wood edge arrives at the present railway.

5. *Go up the stone steps and cross the line with care.* Descending the embankment on the other wise. You are in a local playing field. Turn left along the edge of the railway and then ahead on a track that leads through the gorse into some woodland. The path separates into two, but rejoins in a few metres. Soon afterwards, follow the path that goes to the right and very soon goes left along the edge of the trees, with a fence to the right. Follow this until it emerges on a wide farm track.

Go straight ahead down the unsurfaced road, which is Red Delph Lane. This comes out on the by-pass road. Cross straight over and you are back in Siding Lane.

Walk 20

Rufford (1)

An old hall and a nature reserve are the highspots of this easy walk.

Route: Station – Rufford Old Hall – New Hall – Mere Sands – Station.

Start: Rufford Station. Grid reference: 467 157.

Distance: 3½ or 2½ miles.

Duration: 2½ or 2 hours

Map: SD41/51

By train: Rufford station is on the Ormskirk to Preston line.

By car: Rufford is on the A59. In the centre of the village, turn onto the B5246, signposted to Parbold. Cross the canal bridge, go over the level crossing and parking is on the right.

Refreshments: Hesketh Arms and Rufford Arms. Rufford Hall is open April to October daily 1.00pm – 5.00pm, except Thursdays and Fridays. Mere Sands Wood Visitor Centre is open 9.00am – 5.00pm most days.

1. *From the station walk back over the railway line.* At the canal bridge turn right, along the railings, down onto the canal bank. Ignore a British Waterways warning sign on the bridge by the signpost to Rufford Old Hall. This does not apply to walkers. Just on the other side of the bridge, St Peter's parish church can be seen. As the track meets the tow path, it becomes a

grassy surface and continues through an avenue of trees. The buildings and grounds of the Old Hall soon appear on the opposite bank.

The main entrance for visitors to the Hall is on the A59. It has 14½ acres of grounds and has been National Trust property since 1936. The original donor was Baron Hesketh, whose family seat it was. Inside the house, there is a fine great hall, containing an ornate hammerbeam roof dating from 1485, and a carved wooden screen. Wings were added to the house in 1662 and 1821. In addition, there is the Philip Ashcroft museum of country life. Amongst other things, this reproduces a village kitchen and has a room containing old agricultural instruments. It is well worth making time to spend an hour or so at the Hall.

Along the bank, a swing bridge is reached. Do not cross, but continue on to Spark road bridge in the distance. As the canal passes under the bridge, take the wooden steps on the far side up onto the road. Turn right over the canal and then almost immediately left into Spark Lane. This short road meets the A59 highway at the Rufford Arms Hotel.

2. *On the opposite side of the road is a bridleway,* named Croston Drive. Go along this, passing the houses, until there is an open field on the right and a wood on the left. The trees surround Rufford New Hall, which dates from 1778 and is not open to the public. The wide track makes its way through the outbuildings of Park Farm. Leaving the farm behind keep on along until reaching a junction.

3. *To shorten the walk, at the junction, turn left* along a track, which eventually runs alongside the wood and then to the road. Turn right and then left down the lane, which leads to the Mere Sands car park.

For the longer walk, do not turn left after the farm, but go

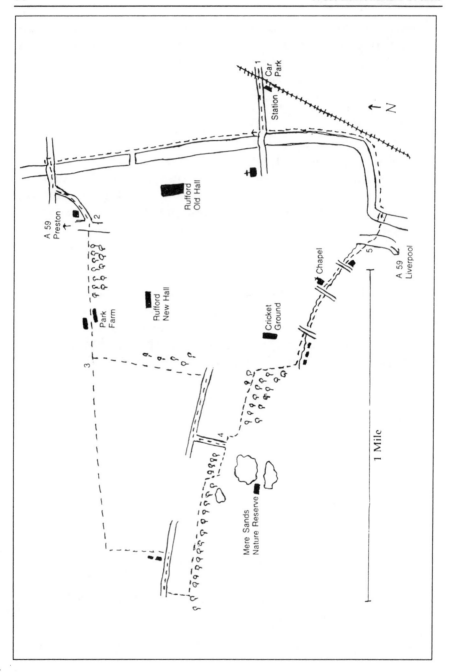

ahead down a long wide track. As the track continues on, turn left along another track, making to the right of a group of trees and a bank, which surrounds a pond. After passing the pond, carry on until the track becomes a wider stone one, with houses to the right. This emerges on the road. Turn right and soon look for a signpost in the hedge on the other side of the road. This takes you straight across a field to a footbridge. This in turn takes you into Mere Sands Wood.

At the end of the short access path, turn left by a sign warning to keep dogs on a lead. The well-used path then wanders for some distance, staying fairly close to the edge of the wood. Ignore all paths to the right. Eventually, there is no option but to turn sharp right with a fence to the left. The barking of dogs tells you that the private kennels are nearby.

The path then swings to the left, by the hide overlooking the lake and comes out in a car park. On the right is a map of the nature reserve, which is run by the Lancashire Trust for Nature Conservation. It's main aim is to protect wild life. The wood covers 105 acres and includes a number of lakes. The trees were originally planted by Lord Hesketh in the middle of the nineteenth century. However, the name 'Mere Sands" comes from centuries earlier, when it stood on the edge of a large lake called Martin Mere. More recently the wood has been a sand quarry, but now it is a lovely area in which to walk or quietly study the wild life. Mere Sands is not to be confused with the Martin Mere bird sanctuary, which is some distance away. It is worth stopping to get a trail leaflet about the wood and its amenities from the visitors' centre. If time allows, it is also worth taking time to go round some of the paths and perhaps spending a little time in one of the hides overlooking the small lakes. These were formed from old quarry pits. The shorter walk joins the longer one here.

4. *Take the path on the opposite side of the car park,* adjacent to the main entrance. It keeps to the edge of the wood, passing

the stile on an access path to the left. As the path ends, turn left out of the wood, along the edge of a stream. This is at first through a field and then Rufford cricket ground. There are houses on the opposite bank. The path comes out onto a narrow road.

Look for the signpost on the other side of the bridge, as the path now runs down the opposite side of the stream, it comes out onto another narrow road and again swaps to the other side of the stream. Look for the signpost on the left-hand side of the bridge, close to the old Methodist chapel, now a conference and retreat centre. At another small road, turn right across the bridge and then left, through the farm yard. Stay as close to the edge of the stream as possible. This usually means at first weaving a way through various items of farm machinery. After these, there is a gap in a mound of earth, which leads along the side of the stream to the A59 bridge.

Methodist Conference Centre

5. *Go up onto the road, turn right and then left* over the canal swing bridge. Walk left along the canal bank to the road bridge and then right back to the station.

Walk 21

Rufford (2)

A walk along canal, river and brook, giving a reminder of how important water navigation was in times gone by.

Route: Station – Prescott Bridge – Station.

Start: Rufford station. Grid reference: 467 157.

Distance: 3½ miles

Duration: 1½ hours.

Map: SD41/51

By train: Rufford station is on the Ormskirk to Preston line.

By car: Rufford is on the A59. In the centre of the village, turn onto the B5246, signposted to Parbold. Cross the canal bridge, go over the level crossing and parking is on the right.

Refreshments: Hesketh Arms in the centre of Rufford.

1. *Go left along the road from the station.* Arriving at the canal bridge, go down the steps to the left onto the tow path. You are now on the Rufford branch of the canal or the Lower Douglas Navigation. This runs the seven miles from Burscough to Tarleton, running into the tidal estuary of the River Douglas. An act of Parliament in 1790 gave the owners of the Liverpool-Leeds canal permission to alter the course of the River Douglas, which we follow later in this walk. Having by

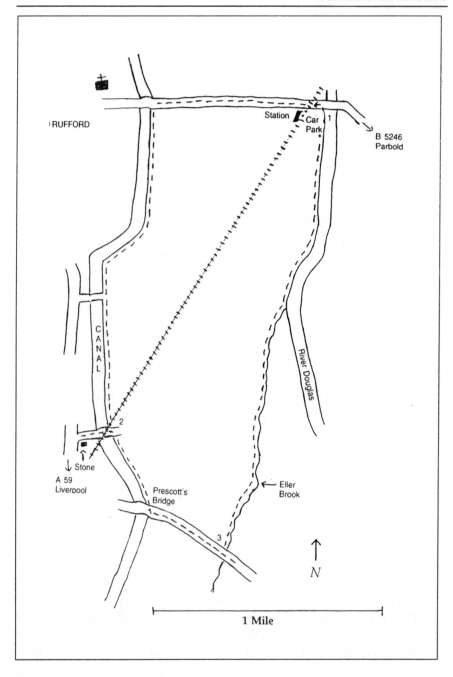

RUFFORD

Station
Car
Park
1

B 5246
Parbold

C
A
N
A
L

River Douglas

2

↓ Stone
A 59
Liverpool

Prescott's
Bridge

← Eller
Brook

3

↑
N

1 Mile

1794 raised suffi-
cient funds, the new
section of canal was
cut, starting at Top
Locks. This section
was known as The
'Rufford Line'. Canal
and river join again
at a lock, north of
Rufford, at Tarleton.
They run parallel to
each other for most
of the length.

Soon arrive at a lock,
which is one of eight
on the Rufford
Branch, namely
Lathom Top and Bot-
tom Locks, Runnel
Brow Lock, Moss,
German's, Bald-
win's, Rufford and

Ancient boundary stone

Tarleton Locks. Besides general commercial goods, the main
cargo of the canal barges was coal. The use of the canal began
to decline in the middle of the nineteenth century with the
arrival of the railways. Since six of these locks are in the first
two miles out of Burscough, this one is the only other one on
the way to Tarleton. The Ormskirk to Preston rail line is
nearby and runs for almost nine miles in a straight line.

2. *The next bridge is a skewbridge.* The canal goes underneath
diagonally and on the bridge itself is a level crossing, carrying
a track across the railway. If you go the short distance to the
right, down the track to the main A59 road, there is an ancient
boundary stone, stating 'Rufford-Leyland Hundred' and
'Lathom-West Derby Hundred'.

Continue along the canal path, until reaching the next bridge, This is Prescott Bridge, built in stone, one of the many on the canal which are named after farmers of the adjoining land at the time of construction. Go to the left to join the lane. (On the other side of the bridge, there are some picnic tables by the canal.) Walk to the left for about 200 metres.

3. *Turn left again.* Go along a wide track to the left of the Eller Brook. Particularly in summer, the cutting and embankment seem very large for a small stream. After about a mile it links up with the River Douglas. Before the cutting of the canal, the River Douglas was the main navigation route. Improvements to it were first undertaken in the 1720s, mainly to improve the transportation of coal from Wigan to Liverpool via the Ribble. Small sailing boats were most probably used, given the shallowness of the river.

On reaching the road bridge at Rufford, leave the river and turn left back to the station.

Walk 22

Rivington

A book of walks in the area missing out Rivington would be incomplete. Although just outside West Lancashire, the reservoirs supply water to Merseyside. Lord Leverhulme's terrace garden has the quiet beauty of a faded glory.

Route: Hall Barn – Terrace Garden – Rivington Pike – Hall Barn.

Start: Great Barn or Hall Barn, Rivington. Grid refs: 628 139 or 634 144.

Distance: 2½ miles (from the Hall Barn), 3 miles from the Great Barn.

Duration: 2 hours or 2½ hours.

Map: SD61/71

By Train: None

By car: Reach the village of Anderton on the A673 between Chorley and Bolton. From the Chorley direction, turn left at the traffic lights in the middle of the village, down Babylon Lane. At the next junction, turn right over the M61. Turn next left into Horrobin Lane. After crossing the reservoir, turn right in Rivington village, following signs for Horwich and Great Barn.

Refreshments: Great Barn.

The name most associated with Rivington is that of Lord Leverhulme. Originally from Bolton, William Lever was a great businessman. The pinnacle of this success came towards the end of the nineteenth century, when he built a factory in Birkenhead to manufacture soap. The place was called Port Sunlight, after the brand name of his soap. As well as the factory, he erected a model village for his workforce. This is unchanged and is well worth a visit. In the first twenty years of the twentieth century, on the wooded slopes below Rivington Pike, he had built a terraced garden containing a fascinating variety of buildings. Leverhulme died a few years after its completion. His name lives on through the giant firm of Unilever. Unfortunately, his work at Rivington was allowed to fall into ruin. A walk round the gardens today gives a nostalgic glimpse into the faded glory of the past.

It is worth calling in at Great House barn before or after the walk. It not only houses a café and information centre with a range of local walks, but also is of historic importance as a building. Both this and Rivington Hall Barn, at the other end of Hall Drive, originate from the eighteenth century. The oak cruck trusses and a few other items are original, but there have been numerous alterations over the years. After years of agricultural use, it was Lord Leverhulme who changed the barns into visitor centres.

Rivington Pike

If you have parked at Great House Barn, then walk up Hall Drive to the Hall. Turn left in front of it, across the bridge and bear right to arrive at the Hall Barn car park.

1. *From the car park, go to the left of the barn and leftwards towards a gate.* The wide stony track begins to ascend, with a gorge to the right. There is an alternative narrow path by the rails on the left, which some find an easier walking surface. At the top of the ascent is an open space to the left. Do not follow the narrower track which goes off to the left, but take the main track, which soon doubles back on itself along the other side of the gorge.

On the left is a stile, which leads to a well-used path going up to the pike, which can be seen above. Keep on the main track and pass through a gate. Avoid the narrow path going to the right. At the next junction of a number of paths, go left through the gate. A red lettered sign points to the Terrace. Go uphill and, at the entrance to the wood, pass through a gate.

2. *This is where the terraced gardens and buildings start.* On the left is the site of South Lodge, the only remaining piece of which is the small stone pillar, on the right just through the gate. Bear right to follow the track as it starts to climb, passing a flight of steps on the left. As a path goes off to the right, keep to the one which continues to climb. Arriving at a junction of six paths, move on to the one to the left of the steeply descending steps. This continues ahead on the level, as the one you are leaving continues to climb ahead. Make a note of this spot, because this is the place to which you will return down the path second left later in the walk.

The path you are now on is paved. After a while, on the right you will see the substantial remains of a garden shelter built on the slope. Continue on to the man-made ravine, crossed by a stone bridge. At the bottom of the ravine is the blue pool. As the path continues on the other side of the ravine, in a few

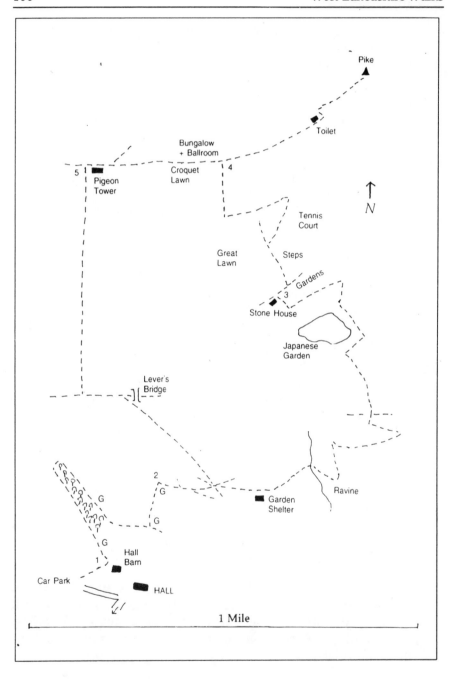

metres go left up the steps, until joining another path at a junction. Turn right. The path eventually turns back on itself to reach Royton Lane.

Cross the lane and up the steps opposite. You are now entering the Japanese Gardens. On the left you will see the remains of the base of a Japanese lantern. As a path goes to the left, turn right through the rhododendron bushes. Then, on your left you will see the large pool, which in former times was much deeper. As the path turns left, note, to the right, the remains of one of the tea houses.

At the top of the path, bear to the right to reach what is left of some buildings connected with the kitchen garden. Turn left in front of these, and walk through the overgrown gardens. One or two cherry trees are about all that indicate its former glory. On the right, pass the dividing walls of the garden, ending with the greenhouse site. At the end of the gardens turn right and find, on the left, the remains of Stone House. All that is to be seen are the cellars, the entrance pillars, and the drive that came up to the house.

3. *Turn right along the wide track and immediately left.* Ascend the steps going up to the archway above. On the flat, beyond the archway, over to the left is the Great Lawn. Here Lord Leverhulme used to hold great gatherings and events. As the steps continue upwards, go round to the right to the tennis court, the outline of which can still be discerned. Then go up the steps of the adjacent building and turn left, passing en route the steps of Long Walk and the back of the building on the Great Lawn.

At the end turn right and go up the steps of big stone slabs. At the top, continue slightly to the right towards the flight of steps to be seen in the distance. The flat area at the top of the steps was the site of the buildings known as the Bungalow and also of the Ballroom. All that remains is some of the floor tiling.

4. *If the walk is to be extended to visit the pike,* follow the sign on the path second to the right at the top of the steps, marked to the Pike and Toilet Block. At the top of the path is a gate and on the left the toilets, built on the site of Bolton Lodge. Beyond the toilets, cross the wide track, turn left for a few metres, and then, right up to the Pike which can be seen above. The tower was built in 1733 and stands 1,200 feet above sea level. From the tower return, by the same route, back to the site of The Bungalow and Ballroom.

Turn left from the steps and walk diagonally across the space. At the far corner, go down the steps on the left to see the site of the old croquet lawn. Back up the steps, turn left along the wide path, passing through the site of the old Belmont Lodge. Through a gate arrive at a junction of wide paths, with Pigeon Tower on the left. Lady Leverhulme used the top floor, with its panoramic views, as her sewing room.

5. *Do not follow the wide track downhill,* but go through the gate in front of the tower, along the front of the building and then to the left. Do not go on to the terraces on the left, but follow the gravel path downhill. As this veers to the right, continue down on the grass path. At the bottom, turn left along the wide track. In front of you will be seen the seven arch Levers Bridge.

Just before the bridge, turn right. Follow this path, with others joining it from both sides all the way, straight downhill. It eventually arrives at the meeting of six paths mentioned earlier in the way. If you try to go straight on you will find yourself going down some steep steps. Instead turn right and follow the opening part of the walk back to the car park.

Walk 23

Skelmersdale (1)

This walk travels from the comparative heights of Ashurst to the valley of Dean Wood.

Route: Beacon Park — Upholland College — Dean Wood — Ayrefield House — Beacon Park.

Start: Beacon Country Park. Grid Ref: 506 067.

Distance: 4½ miles.

Duration: 2 hours.

Map: SD40/50

By train: None.

By car: Follow the sign to the right off the A5209 Burscough to Parbold road, just east of the village of Newburgh. The park is 1½ miles further on.

Refreshments: Beacon Park Centre and The Fox, Roby Mill.

---

1. *Walk up the hill, away from the car-park and club house.* Aim for the left corner of the woods ahead. Do not go on the path to the left, towards the road, but on the one that goes through the short stretch of woods ahead to a car park. From here, go right along the road, until reaching a signposted turning to the left. This is a wide track, which descends downhill.

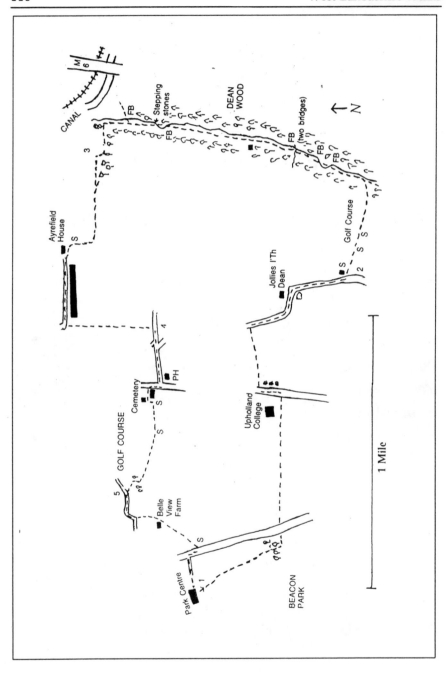

At the bottom of the descent, carry straight on following the path that leads through the centre of the farm. This soon joins a metal road, which comes in from the left from Upholland College. Go straight down the road, with the College on the left and fields to the right. St Joseph's Roman Catholic College was opened in 1883. It has been a seminary for young people training for the priesthood. With the fall in such vocations, it is now used as a conference and training centre for the church.

Upholland College

On arriving at the main road. Turn left past the entrance to the college. After the bungalows on the right-hand side, there is a sign to the right. Follow the track down hill to the left of the fence and then across the field, following the line of poles, to come out on Lafford Lane. Turn right along the lane, passing on the left the quaintly named Jollies i' the Dean Farm. The road bends to the left and then sharply to the right, with a pond on the corner. Starting to go uphill, pass the house with the wide drive on the left and, a little further up the incline, turn left at a signpost. This is by the gate with a red box on it.

2. *The path goes to the left behind the hedge for a short distance.* Then go right over the stile and walk along the edge of the field, passing over two more stiles. After the final one, there is a choice of ways. Ignore all tracks to the right and left. Go ahead slightly to the right of the bushes, between two white posts onto the path that leads into the trees. Do not take the footbridge to the left, but follow the signpost ahead. As the main path goes to the right, go on the narrower path ahead that descends quickly to the valley below. It swings to the right to a junction. This is Dean Wood, where much work has been done over the past few years by the Friends of Dean Wood to improve the footpaths.

Go sharp left, keeping to the edge of the stream. This is a particularly beautiful part of the walk, but can be muddy most of the year round. Continue, with the stream to the right, crossing a bridge across a small tributary. Sections of the path here are lined by a log border. The path crosses a loop in the stream by means of a bridge and, after a few metres, returns to the left of the stream by means of another bridge. There is a short board walk and an incline of log steps, before arriving at a double footbridge. Cross the first one over a tributary to the main stream, but not the second. Continue, with the stream still on the right.

After crossing another tributary bridge, arrive at some steps going up to the left. Although this would seem to be the main path, keep to the less obvious one by the side of the stream. Pass some more steps coming down from the left and go over the log fallen across the path. This has had a piece cut out of it for the convenience of walkers. Go past the remains of an old building on the left. The path then rises a little above the stream, by means of steps. A few metres on, ignore the path to the left and take the one back to the side of the stream. Some steps again take the path upwards. As it rises, look out for steps going steeply back down to the stream. They are easy to miss. At the foot of the steps, cross the bridge to the other side of the stream. Soon, the path returns to the left side of the stream over stepping stones.

Follow the path until reaching a footbridge across the stream. A one minute detour across the bridge will reveal three means of transport, the M6 viaduct, the railway and the canal, in close proximity. Come back across the bridge and turn right, with the stream on the right. Soon you will see the River Douglas to the right. The path then goes to the left, alongside a fence, continuing round to the right. The path then rises away from the fence, through the gorse.

3. *At the stile on the left, go onto the sunken farm track,* which soon rises and continues on a long steady curve to the right. Staying with the ditch and a straggle of trees to the right, pass a pond. The track at length swings more sharply to the right towards Ayrefield House. There are good views from this point, with Winter Hill away to the right and Up Holland College on the skyline to the left. Just before Ayrefield House, go through the wicket gate and bear left round the pond. After following the short track between low stone walls, arrive at the lane through the gap by the gate.

Turn left along the lane. The stone track eventually becomes a metal one, with a long row of houses on the left side. As the road goes sharply to the right, a signpost on the left leads the way to a path between wooden fences. It comes out into a field. Descend, keeping to the left of the hedge. At the bottom of the field, the path continues ahead through the middle of another field and then there is a short uphill section which will bring you on to the road, alongside a bungalow.

4. *Turn right, passing St Gabriel's Close on the right* and Lafford Lane on the left. Passing Roby Mill CE School on the right,

come to a T-Junction, with the Fox Inn on the corner. Turn right and almost immediately, on the left, is a footpath sign. As you go forward a few metres by the side of the house, the cemetery car park is on the right. Then follow the path another few metres to the left and go right through the gate. Keep the hedge to the left, gradually going uphill. After the stile, there is a hedge running up the hill. Keep to the left of this until the clump of trees on the right. Follow round to the right. Then soon go to the left, aiming for a stile in the hedge, to the right of the house on the opposite side of the golf course.

5. *Go left up the narrow road, passing the Dalton sign.* Do not turn along the signed track to the right, but follow the road round the bend. After Crisp Cottage, there is a track to the left, as the road bears to the right. Go through the gap by the gate, and follow the track uphill. Pass through the centres of the deserted and dilapidated Belle View Farm.

Beyond the farm, bear right by the gate. Follow the path through moorland, with the boundary to the right. After the moorland, the way is along the left edge of the adjacent field. At the end of the field, go over the stile onto the road. Turn right and then left into Beacon Park.

Walk 24

Skelmersdale (2)

An undulating walk around the higher ground above
Skelmersdale with good views of the surrounding countryside.

Route: Beacon Park – Ashurst's Beacon – Stonehall – Beacon Park.

Start: Beacon Country Park: Grid reference: 506 067

Distance: 4 or 2½ miles.

Duration: 1½ or 1 hour.

Map: SD40/50

By train: None

By car: Reach the car park by following the sign off the A5209 just east of Newburgh.

Refreshments: Beacon Park Centre; Beacon Inn, Dalton.

---

1. *From the car park,* walk towards the entrance to the first tee on the golf course., The path is to the left of the hedge and then to the right of the next short section of hedge. Aim for the left corner of the copse ahead. Walk to the right along the front edge of the trees. Take the path on the left that goes through the wood. Keep ahead at the crossroad of paths to emerge on the golf course.

Turn right through the avenue of trees. After the second cross path, the trees to the left stop. At the third cross path, take the path into the wood, by the white lime trees. In the wood, go ahead at the crossing of paths. Ignoring paths to the right. Keep on until reaching a small car park.

Ashurst's Beacon

2. *Leaving the car park,* turn right for a short way up the road. Just before the Beacon Inn, take the wide track on the left, through the gate. From the path it is possible to see Ashurst's Beacon just ahead. Soon the ways split, one track going ahead, the other bearing left towards the beacon, from where there are fine views over Skelmersdale and into the distance. On the tower itself, a plaque states that the land was bought by the wife of a Wigan journalist as a memorial to his love of the area. The beacon tower was re-erected in 1798 by Lord Skelmersdale, when it was thought that a French invasion was about to take place. Look outs were on duty ready to light the fire, if the enemy landed.

From the beacon, bear right towards a well-worn hillock. Follow the path down the other side into the trees. On meeting another path, walk to the right until reaching a gate and stile on the left. Over the stile, bear right and descend downhill,

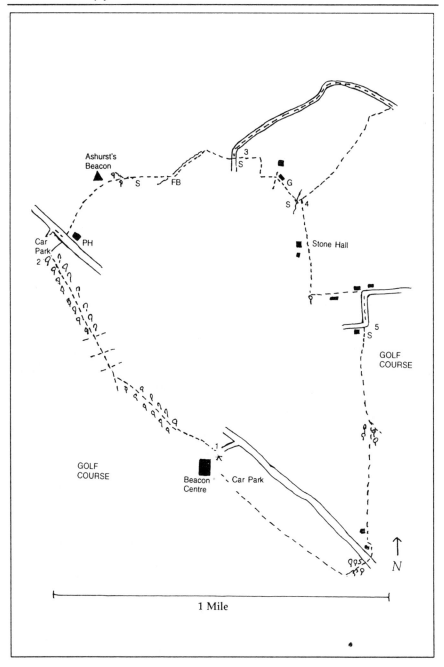

Ashurst's Beacon

FB

Car Park 2

PH

Stone Hall

GOLF COURSE

GOLF COURSE

Beacon Centre   Car Park

N

1 Mile

keeping close to the trees and fence. Turn right by a stile and then descend sharply to a stream and cross the footbridge. On the other side, keep the stream to the left and then turn at right angles along a hedge to descend to the narrow road.

3. *For the shorter walk,* follow the sign on the opposite side of the road. Over the stile continue along the left edge of the field, and at the corner of the field, turn right and continue uphill, still at the edge of the field. Arriving at a metal track, turn left. Cross over the wide track leading to the house on the left. Aim slightly right to the back of the shed. The path continues over a gate and then descends down a grass alleyway. Bending to the right, this reaches a stream, on the other side of which is a stile. The path then ascends to a wide farm track, where you re-join the longer walk.

For the longer walk, follow the narrow road down hill for a mile. This is a peaceful stretch, with some fine renovated cottages to admire. Do not turn off at any point. Eventually the metal road ends. There is a house on the left. Ignore the path directly ahead. Follow the one that starts to go uphill to the right. This is an ancient stone way, which continues upwards, with the stream to the right.

At the top of the hill, the track bends to the left and the top of the climb has been reached.

4. *Here, the shorter and longer walk join.* Continue along through the farm at Stonehouse, with the house itself and then a bungalow on the right. Beyond the bungalow, the track comes to a junction, with a tree as a marker. Turn left and follow the track past a cottage on the right, meeting the road by another bungalow. Here, turn right. Then, as the road bends to the right, look for a stile on the left.

5. *Over the stile, turn sharply right* and keep to the hedge and trees in front of the house. On the left is the golf course.

Keep ahead, keeping close to the wall and hedge. On the left is now a large open field. When the end of this is reached, resist the temptation to march straight on. Instead, take a path bearing right, which wanders for a distance through a wooded glade. This comes out into a field. Keeping to the right edge, pass a house on the right. The path then becomes enclosed and swings right round an old cottage to reach the road.

Across the road is a footpath sign. Go over the stile and through the trees. Turn right and walk across the middle of the large open space. You are back in Beacon Park. The Park Centre is soon in sight and the car park only a short distance ahead.

Walk 25

Sollom

The villages of Sollom and Tarleton, as well as the Bank Hall Estate are included in this walk never far away from canal and river.

Route: Sollom – Red Bridge – Bank Hall- Tarleton – Sollom.

Start: The small village of Sollom. Grid reference: 455 187

Distance: 5 miles.

Duration: 2½ hours.

Map: SD42/52 and SD41/51.

By train: None

By car: There is room to park on the right-hand side of the road opposite to Green Lane Farm, immediately after coming off the A59.

Refreshments: Lord Lilford and Cock and Bootle public houses in Tarleton, plus Quincey's grill bar at junction of the A59 and A565.

1. *Our starting point of Sollom is a little village* that most people rush by on the A59 by-pass, unaware of its existence. It is now a quiet spot, but a couple of centuries ago, it was a busy place. It grew originally as a canal village, with a pub and cottages close to the lock. It linked the canal transport system to the Great North Road, which ran through the centre of the village. It is difficult to imagine the hustle and bustle of early days.

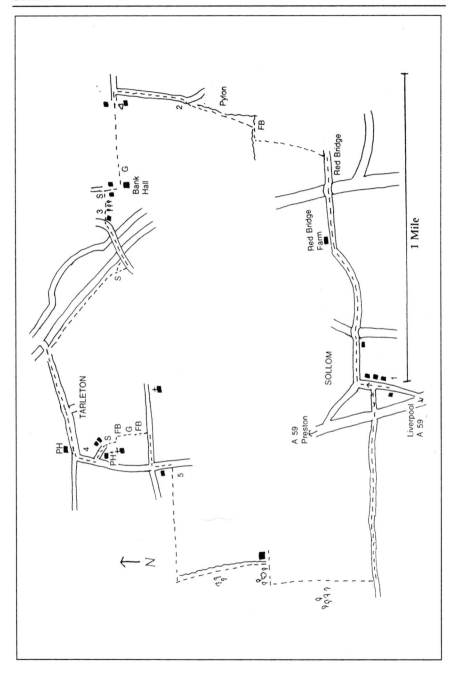

The racehorse sign, on the left as you enter the village from the A59, is a reminder that further down the road are the stables. It was here, in 1980 that Captain Wilson's daughter, Geraldine, went to Aintree to be the first woman to finish in a Grand National.

Walk away from the A59 and turn right down Lock Lane. Pass Lock House on the right and go over the bridge. Here was the lock and this was the final point on the Rufford Branch of the Leeds and Liverpool canal. On the other side of the bridge, can be seen the old course of the River Douglas.

Over the bridge, follow the metal road ahead. It bends to the left for a little while. There is a stone track, which soon, for some reason, reverts to tarmac. Pass Red Bridge Farm, with its little pond, on the left. This is now a kennels. At Red Bridge, look south to see the joint tributary of the Rivers Lostock and Yarrow, coming in from the left.

Continue along the lane for a few metres. Almost immediately, on the left, is a large field, with ditches around the edges. Turn left through the wide gap in the hedge and head just to the left of the footbridge in the distance ahead. At the stream, turn right for a few metres and go over the bridge. The line of the right of way is not around the edge of the stream to the right, but at an angle to meet the ditch about halfway between the right corner of the field and the large electricity pylon.

From the pylon, continue along the edge of the ditch. At the corner of the field, turn right down the wide track back onto the lane.

2. *Walk left along the lane, passing the occasional house en route.* After a white house with pond on the left, the lane veers to the right. Here, turn left at the footpath sign, by the lodge house. Carry on down the metal path through the trees. Do not be put off by the private road notices. It is still a right of way for walkers.

All this area is part of the Bank Hall Estate. Pass the kindergarten on the right and go through the small gate, by the larger gate. Ignore all tracks to the right or left, most of which have warning notices. At the end of the lane, to the left, are the dilapidated remains of Bank Hall. In former years this was the home of Lord Lilford. Now conservation groups are trying to save the hall, before it is completely beyond repair.

Turn right and walk on the wide paved track through the middle of the farm. After passing the barn on the left and just as the lane begins, there is a stile on the left. Follow the path along the edge of the trees to the A59.

The Old Mill at Tarleton Bridge

3. *Here, go left along the road, passing a lodge on the left.* The road bridge goes over the River Douglas and another stretch of canal. On the other side of the bridge, cross the road. Be very careful indeed, because this is a dangerous stretch. On

the other side of the road, there is a choice of going down to
the canal by means of the steps through the narrow gap. Or,
a few metres to the left, go through the much wider gap onto
a track. The short path from the canal joins this track from the
right after a short while. On the opposite bank of the canal is
an imposing old mill building.

The track comes to two stiles by the side of the canal. These
lead into a field. The path goes along the edge of the canal,
until it goes by fencing to the left and onto the concrete road
in front of the small industrial estate. Go along in front of the
buildings. With a bridge on the right, turn left up the road,
passing an old farm dated 1655 on the right. At the end of the
road, go straight ahead, ignoring the road to the left and the
one to the right, marked Hesketh Bank.

4. *After passing the Lord Lilford pub on the right,* the road bears
to the left. Just before the Cock and Bottle pub on the left,
follow the signpost down the lane. As the lane ends, in the
right corner, is a stile. The path goes along the back of the
church grounds and then left to a junction with another path.
The bridge over the stream here must be unique, because it is
an old gravestone. Turn right along the path. Go through the
old kissing gate into a field. Keep to the left of the field edge.
Looking across to the left, the old historic church of Tarleton
can be seen. This was replaced by the new one in Tarleton
village centre. Services are now held in the old one once a
year. After going over a footbridge, reach the A59 once more.

Cross the road and turn right. Pass in front of Animal World,
where it is possible to buy all sorts of exotic creatures. Bear
left alongside the A59, with Quincey's grill bar on the left.
This building dates from 1640 and was until recent times the
Rams Head, an old coaching inn. Cross to the other side of the
A59. Turn left, passing a house, and, at the end of the hedge,
turn right to the sign.

5. *This takes you along a wide farm track.* Pass the first ditch on the left. At the second, turn left along the right-hand side of the ditch.

After crossing the field, the path for a short way follows a hedge to the left. Follow the path through the trees and continue, with the ditch on the left, along the next field. The path ends as it comes to a lane, with a house to the left. Turn right along the lane, passing the copse and pond on the right. After the copse, look for the sign to the left. Go straight towards the left edge of the wood. A notice warns to keep to the path, which goes forward through the wood. Emerging from it, the path continues to a metal road.

Turn left and follow the road until it reaches the A59, yet again. Cross the road and go down the short stretch of lane back into Sollom.

More Walks in the North-West!

CHESHIRE WALKS

· with children ·

Nick Lambert

Cheshire Walks with Children

"If only my children were interested in walking," They will be with the help of this book by Nick Lambert! Easy to follow directions for mums & dads, plus lots of interesting things to see along the way. There are even some routes suitable for push chairs and all are on well-maintained paths that are easily negotiated by little people.

£6.95

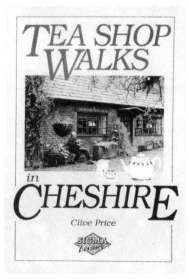

TEA SHOP WALKS IN CHESHIRE

Walk a few miles in Cheshire, then reward yourself with a leisurely afternoon tea in one of the county's many and varied tea shops. Clive Price has selected some of the most attractive walks in the area and a wide range of tea shops ranging from a station waiting room to a medieval monastic refectory!

£6.95

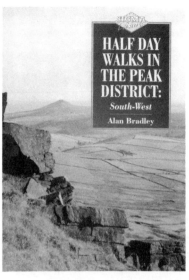

HALF-DAY WALKS IN THE PEAK DISTRICT: South West

Alan Bradley has devised a wide range of walks that all fit into a half day - suitable for families with small children, those with little time to spare or the just plain lazy! Clear sketch maps and choices of starting points give great flexibility - and you can easily join routes together for longer expeditions.

£6.95

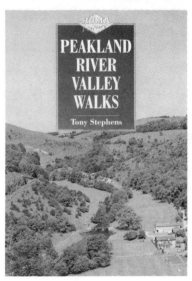

PEAKLAND RIVER VALLEY WALKS

Tony Stephens has researched some 200 miles of walks along almost 20 rivers plus countless tributaries and canals to devise this authoritative book. There are walks from 8 to 33 miles with frequent detours to places of interest plus notes on the geology, flora and history of the places you visit.

£7.95

We publish guides to individual towns, plus books on walking and cycling in the great outdoors throughout England and Wales. This is a recent selection:

The Lake District

TEA SHOP WALKS IN THE LAKE DISTRICT – Jean Patefield *(£6.95)*

WALKING LAKELAND TRACKWAYS: the Eastern Lakes – Mike Creswell *(£7.95)*

THE LAKELAND SUMMITS: a survey of the fells of the Lake District National Park – Tim Synge *(£7.95)*

FULL DAYS ON THE FELLS – Adrian Dixon *(£7.95)*

100 LAKE DISTRICT HILL WALKS – Gordon Brown *(£7.95)*

LAKELAND ROCKY RAMBLES: Geology beneath your feet – Brian Lynas *(£9.95)*

PUB WALKS IN THE LAKE DISTRICT – Neil Coates *(£6.95)*

LAKELAND WALKING, ON THE LEVEL – Norman Buckley *(£6.95)*

MOSTLY DOWNHILL: LEISURELY WALKS IN THE LAKE DISTRICT – Alan Pears *(£6.95)*

THE THIRLMERE WAY – Tim Cappelli *(£6.95)*

CYCLING IN THE LAKE DISTRICT – John Wood *(£7.95)*

Other destinations . . .

FIFTY CLASSIC WALKS IN THE PENNINES – Terry Marsh *(£8.95)*

EAST CHESHIRE WALKS – Graham Beech *(£5.95)*

RAMBLES AROUND MANCHESTER – Mike Cresswell *(£5.95)*

YORKSHIRE DALES WALKING: On The Level –
Norman Buckley *(£6.95)*

WALKS IN MYSTERIOUS WALES – Laurence Main *(£7.95)*

CHALLENGING WALKS: NW England & N Wales –
Ron Astley *(£7.95)*

BEST PUB WALKS – CHESTER & THE DEE VALLEY –
John Haywood *(£6.95)*

BEST PUB WALKS IN GWENT – Les Lumsdon *(£6.95)*

BEST PUB WALKS IN POWYS – Les Lumsdon & Chris
Rushton *(£6.95)*

BEST PUB WALKS IN PEMBROKESHIRE – Laurence Main
(£6.95)

BEST PUB WALKS IN THE NORTH PENNINES –
Nick Channer *(£6.95)*

LOG BOOK OF THE MOUNTAINS OF ENGLAND –
Mark Woosey *(£9.95)*

LOG BOOK OF THE MOUNTAINS OF WALES –
Mark Woosey *(£7.95)*

There are many more titles in our fabulous series of 'Best
Pub Walks' books for just about every popular walking
area in the UK, all featuring access by public transport.All
of our books are available from your local bookshop. In
case of difficulty, or to obtain our complete catalogue,
please contact:

SIGMA LEISURE, 1 SOUTH OAK LANE, WILMSLOW, CHESHIRE SK9 6AR
Phone: 01625 – 531035   Fax: 01625 – 536800

ACCESS and VISA orders welcome – call our friendly sales staff or
use our 24 hour Answerphone service! Most orders are despatched
on the day we receive your order – you could be enjoying our books in
just a couple of days. Please add £2 p&p to all orders.